D1367796

IT'S BASIC INCOME

The Global Debate

Edited by Amy Downes and Stewart Lansley

First published in Great Britain in 2018 by

Policy Press
University of Bristol
1-9 Old Park Hill
Bristol
BS2 8BB
UK
t: +44 (0)117 954 5940
pp-info@bristol.ac.uk
www.policypress.co.uk

North America office:
Policy Press
c/o The University of Chicago Press
1427 East 60th Street
Chicago, IL 60637, USA
t: +1 773 702 7700
f: +1 773 702 9756
sales@press.uchicago.edu
www.press.uchicago.edu

© Policy Press 2018

British Library Cataloguing in Publication Data
A catalogue record for this book is available from the British Library.

Library of Congress Cataloging-in-Publication Data
A catalog record for this book has been requested.

ISBN 978-1-4473-4390-5 paperback
ISBN 978-1-4473-3392-9 ePub
ISBN 978-1-4473-3393-6 Mobi
ISBN 978-1-4473-3391-2 ePdf

It's Basic Income is a project designed by Work till Late
Book design by Work till Late
Special thanks to Jules Estèves for permission to use the typeface 'Brill' for this project
Printed and bound in Great Britain by TJ International, Padstow
Policy Press uses environmentally responsible print partners

Contents

Contents

Contents

Part VI: The way forward

The contributors

Bruna Augusto is a biologist, President of ReCivitas and co-founder of the Brazilian Pilot Project of Basic Income at Quatinga Velho.

Ursula Barry is Associate Professor with the School of Social Policy, Social Work and Social Justice, University College Dublin. She is the Irish representative on the EU Expert Network SAAGE (Scientific Analysis and Assessment on Gender Equality).

Jonathan Bartley is co-leader of the UK Green Party and a disability rights campaigner. He was vice-chair of the Electoral Reform Society and served as chair of the Centre for Studies on Inclusive Education.

Roderick Benns is the editor of The Case for Basic Income news site and publisher of *The Lindsay Advocate*, a community newspaper focused on Lindsay's basic income pilot. He is a member of the Basic Income Canada Network.

Peter Beresford OBE is Professor of Citizen Participation at the University of Essex, Emeritus Professor of Social Policy at Brunel University London and Co-Chair of Shaping Our Lives, a national disabled people's organisation.

Marcus Brancaglione is a basic income and direct democracy activist, founder of ReCivitas and co-founder of the Brazilian Pilot Project of Basic Income at Quatinga Velho (2008-14), recently resumed (2016) as Startup.

Brenton Caffin is Director of Innovation Skills at London-based Nesta. He advises national and global organisations on issues relating to social and public sector innovation.

Sarath Davala is a development sociologist and co-founder and coordinator of the India Network for Basic Income. He researches, writes about and advocates unconditional basic income as an alternative social policy.

Toby Deller is a freelance viola player and writer. He is the author of 'The arts world should look outside itself and campaign for universal basic income', rhinegold.co.uk, April 2016.

Alexander de Roo is Chairman of the Dutch branch of the Basic Income Earth Network, co-founder and former Treasurer of BIEN; co-founder of the Dutch Green Party and former Member of the European Parliament.

Amy Downes is a designer and co-founder of UK creative agency Work till Late. She studied philosophy at University College London, writing her Master's thesis on the subject of unconditional basic income in 2009.

Eight – the Belgium-based crowd-funded charity Eight was founded by philosopher/documentary filmmaker Steven Janssens and sociologist/development aid expert Maarten Goethals. Eight is looking for ways to reduce inequality in the world and has created a model that is a combination of scarcity theory and basic income.

Uffe Elbæk is the leader of Alternativet, Denmark's progressive green party, which he formed in 2013. He is a former Minister of Culture under Helle Thorning Schmidt's centre-left government. Alternativet now has chapters in other countries including the UK. For more detail about the party, see alternativet.dk.

Brian Eno is an English musician, composer, producer, writer and visual artist. He is best known for his pioneering work in rock, ambient, pop and electronic music.

Martin Ford is a futurist, the founder of a Silicon Valley software development firm and the author of *Rise of the Robots: Technology and the Threat of a Jobless Future*, Oneworld Publications, 2015.

GiveDirectly is a non-profit organisation operating in East Africa that helps families living in extreme poverty by making unconditional cash transfers to them via mobile phone.

Ian Gough is Visiting Professor at the Centre for the Analysis of Social Exclusion, London School of Economics, Associate at the Grantham Research Institute on Climate Change and the Environment (also LSE) and Emeritus Professor of Social Policy at University of Bath.

Louise Haagh is Reader in Politics, University of York. She is chair of the Basic Income Earth Network and co-Editor-in-Chief of *Basic Income Studies*.

Olivia Hanks is a freelance writer and editor and works in local government. She writes for Norwich Radical, a collective of writers providing progressive analysis of politics and the arts.

Andrew Harrop is general secretary of the UK Fabian Society. He is the author of *For us all: Redesigning Social Security, for the 2020s*, Fabian Society, 2016.

Anke Hassel is Professor of Public Policy at the Hertie School of Governance, Berlin and Academic Director of the Hans Böckler Foundation's Institute of Economic and Social Research, Düsseldorf.

Steven Janssens is a Belgian philosopher, documentary filmmaker and founder of Eight, which is currently running a basic income pilot in Uganda.

Soumya Kapoor Mehta is a development economist from Cambridge University. She is co-author, with Sarath Davala, Guy Standing and Renana Jhabvala, of *Basic Income - A Transformative Policy for India*, Bloomsbury, 2015.

Stewart Lansley is a Compass Associate and a visiting fellow at London's City University. He is the author of *A Universal Basic Income*, Compass, 2016 (with Howard Reed), and *A Sharing Economy*, Policy Press, 2016.

Otto Lehto is currently writing his PhD thesis on universal basic income, freedom and property rights at King's College London. He is the former chairman of BIEN Finland (2015-16); ottolehto.com.

Avi Lewis is the director of the feature documentaries *This Changes Everything*, 2015, and *The Take*, 2004, and one of the authors of Canada's *The Leap Manifesto*.

Ruth Lister CBE is a Labour peer and Emeritus Professor of Social Policy at Loughborough University. She chairs the Compass management committee and is a former director of the Child Poverty Action Group.

Caroline Lucas MP is co-leader of the UK Green Party and is Member of Parliament for Brighton Pavilion.

Katie McKenna is one of the lead organisers of Canada's *The Leap Manifesto*, engagement lead for the This Changes Everything project, and a co-producer of the documentary of the same name.

Francine Mestrum is a Brussels-based researcher, international consultant and activist who works mainly on poverty and inequality, social development and globalisation. She is chairwoman of Global Social Justice.

Annie Miller is a co-founder of the Basic Income Earth Network and of Citizen's Basic Income Network Scotland. She is author of *A Basic Income Handbook*, Luath Press, 2017.

Roope Mokka is the founder of independent think-tank, Demos Helsinki. He is a futurist and expert on societal changes and innovation.

Chris Oestereich is a writer, publisher, and zero waste practitioner. He founded the Wicked Problems Collaborative, an American affiliation of members that are tackling some of humanity's biggest issues.

Vanessa Olorenshaw is a writer, founding member of the Women's Equality Party UK and author of *Liberating Motherhood, Birthing the Purplestockings Movement*, Womancraft Publishing, 2016.

Anthony Painter is Director of the Action and Research Centre at the Royal Society of Arts, London, and co-author of *Creative Citizen, Creative State: the principled and pragmatic case for a Universal Basic Income*, RSA, 2015.

Katariina Rantanen is a social policy Master's student at the University of Oxford. She has previously worked at Demos Helsinki as a research assistant.

Howard Reed is a Compass Associate and Director of the UK economic consultancy, Landman Economics (landman-economics.co.uk). He is the author, with Stewart Lansley, of *A Universal Basic Income: An Idea Whose Time Has Come*, Compass, 2016.

Jonathan Reynolds MP is a British Labour Co-operative politician and Shadow Economic Secretary to the Treasury. He leads the Labour Party's working group on basic income.

Elizabeth Rhodes is the Research Director for the Basic Income Study at Y Combinator's 'YC Research', California.

Eduardo Rodriguez-Montemayor is part of the Economics Department at Paris-based INSEAD and a Senior Research Fellow of INSEAD's European Competitiveness Initiative.

The Leap Manifesto is a political manifesto issued by a coalition of Canadian authors, artists, national leaders and activists calling for a restructuring of the Canadian economy and an end to the use of fossil fuels.

The ReCivitas Institute is a Brazilian NGO that works on human rights and public policies. It established the Unconditional Basic Income pilot project in Quatinga Velho, Brazil, which began in 2008.

Malcolm Torry is Director of Citizen's Basic Income Trust and Co-Secretary of the Basic Income Earth Network. He is the author of *The Feasibility of Citizen's Income*, Palgrave, 2016, and *Money for Everyone: Why We Need a Citizen's Income*, Policy Press, 2013.

Jenna van Draanen is a public health practitioner, researcher and evaluator dedicated to social justice, health and wellbeing. She is a Postdoctoral Scholar at The University of British Columbia and a member of the Basic Income Canada Network.

Philippe Van Parijs directs the Hoover Chair of Economic and Social Ethics at the University of Louvain. His books include *What's Wrong with a Free Lunch?*, Beacon Press, 2001, and *Basic Income: A Radical Proposal for a Free Society and a Sane Economy*, Harvard University Press, 2017 (with Yannick Vanderborght).

Karl Widerquist is a political philosopher and economist at Georgetown University-Qatar. He is the co-founder of the US Basic Income Guarantee Network, co-chair of the Basic Income Earth Network and co-founder of *Basic Income News*.

Ed Whitfield is co-founder and Co-Managing Director of the US Fund for Democratic Communities.

Y Combinator is an American seed accelerator providing early stage funding for start-ups. Its not-for-profit arm is YC Research, which is carrying out a small Californian-based pilot on basic income.

Matt Zwolinski is an Associate Professor of Philosophy at the University of San Diego, Co-Director of USD's Institute for Law and Philosophy, and executive director of USD's Center for Ethics, Economics, and Public Policy. He is currently writing a book on the libertarian case for a basic income.

Acknowledgements

The editors would like to thank all those people and organisations that have helped to make this book possible. Sincere thanks go to contributors for taking the time to write a submission and for patience during the editing and production process, especially in responding to queries and meeting deadlines. Thanks too to the editors of *Social Europe* and *openDemocracy* for permission to reproduce articles originally published in their online journals and to *Compass* for permission to reproduce one of their online blogs. A special thanks also to Laura Vickers at Policy Press for belief in the project and support and guidance throughout, and to the wider team at Policy Press for making this book a reality.

Finally, thanks go to friends and colleagues for endless discussion about the basic income debate. Special thanks go to Jonas, whose idea this book was, and who has supported the project wholeheartedly from the start, thank you for your ideas, creativity and belief; to Kirsten who helped turn a mass of articles into a viable publishing proposal; to Daniel who saw value in the project and helped create an identity for it; and to Anne for loyalty, support and insights throughout.

Introduction

Amy Downes and Stewart Lansley, UK

A few years ago, the idea of a universal basic income was widely dismissed as eccentric, as little more than a utopian pipedream. Since then, there has been a significant upsurge in interest, taking the idea from the fringes and up the political agenda in a number of countries.

A universal basic income (UBI) would see a tax-free, unconditional and non-contributory weekly income paid to every individual as of right, irrespective of how much they earned or their work status. Aimed at guaranteeing a no-strings-attached minimum, secure income for all, whatever their circumstances, a UBI would aim to replace at least part of existing national social security systems and would involve a profound revolution in the way income support is organised in most countries.

In the case of the UK, it would constitute a significant extension of the universal model of welfare and, by lowering dependency on means-tested benefits, would relieve the problems of low take-up, the poverty trap and stigma associated with the current system.[1] It would be cheaper to administer, and would save large sums currently spent on processing claims, policing benefit claimants and assessing eligibility.

The idea of a UBI has a long pedigree. The earliest known debate on its essential principles came in 483BC with the discovery of a rich seam of silver in ancient Athenia. The find triggered an intense public discussion about how the potential revenue stream should be spent. One proposal was that it should be distributed among all 30,000 citizens in a regular and equal citizen's dividend, a move that would have transformed the nature of Athenian society. In the event, the Athenian Assembly voted against the path-breaking idea and, instead, the windfall was used to expand the Athenian navy.[2]

In 1516, the social philosopher, Thomas More, floated the idea of a regular basic income as of right in his fictional fantasy Utopia. In 1797 the British-born champion of democracy, Thomas Paine, called for every person to be paid, at the age of 21, a sum of £15 and for those over 50, the sum of £10. 'It is a right', he emphasised, 'and not a charity'.[3] This sum, he argued, would come from a national fund financed from a charge on the ownership of land, thereby ensuring that part of the benefit of that ownership would be shared among all citizens.

Over the last century, a long list of leading economists, politicians and campaigners, of diverse views, have backed some form of basic income. They include Bertrand Russell, James Meade, JK Galbraith, Friedrich von Hayek, Martin Luther King Jr, Paul Samuelson, James Tobin, Milton Friedman and Charles Murray, a list that includes six Nobel laureates. More recently, Barack Obama has said it will be a central policy debate of the next two decades, while a host of Silicon Valley business magnates – including Facebook's Mark Zuckerberg – are also converts, some of them backing it through their own pockets. Sam Altman, head of the start-up incubator Y Combinator, is financing a UBI experiment in California and eBay founder Pierre Omidyar, is investing $500,000 in an experiment in Kenya.

Significantly, and unusually for such a radical idea, UBI has gained support from pro-marketeers such as Hayek and Friedman as well as social democratic egalitarians such as Meade and Galbraith. In the UK there is longstanding support from the Green Party while the 2016 SNP conference gave it backing and the Labour Party is studying its potential.

The current groundswell of support follows a number of earlier waves of interest. The first of these came after the First World War with several UK thinkers calling for some version of a basic income as a way of tackling the severe economic insecurity of the inter-war years.

The next wave came in the second half of the 1960s in response to the call in the United States for a negative income tax (NIT) system by Milton Friedman. NIT and basic income are very different concepts. While a basic income is guaranteed, non-deductible and paid to individuals, a NIT is a means-tested system, paid to households and operated through the tax system. Nevertheless, both can deliver identical or very similar results, though through very different mechanisms, and embracing different underlying philosophies. A proposal for a form of NIT came very close to being implemented by President Richard Nixon in 1972. In the 1970s, there were four trials of local NIT schemes in the US, and one in Canada called Mincome. The third wave followed the 1986 formation of the cross-European (and later cross-world) network of supporters – BIEN (the Basic Income Earth Network) – which helped to build a basic income movement that spanned countries.[4]

Despite the ongoing interest, and two further trials – in Namibia in 2009 and in India from 2009-13 – only two variants of a scheme have been implemented on a permanent basis: in the state of Alaska in the early 1980s and in Iran in 2010. These offer very contrasting approaches, and both were implemented under somewhat special circumstances. Alaska has paid an equal annual social dividend (from $400-$2,000) to all citizens for the last 30 years, effectively implementing a variant of the idea floated in Athens 2,500 years ago and paid for from an oil-financed permanent wealth fund. Although this 'social dividend' approach – known as the 'third rail of Alaskan politics' – takes the form of an annual and not a weekly or monthly payment, it has proved hugely popular and, significantly, has helped ensure that Alaska is one of the most equal of US states.[5] In 2010, Iran adopted an alternative approach – a nationwide, if modest, basic income also financed from oil revenues. The scheme was introduced to compensate for the withdrawal of generous fuel price subsidies.[6]

Nevertheless, despite the limited application to date, the principle of making payments to citizens as of right already exists in many social security systems. In the UK, child benefit is, in essence, a basic income for children.[7] The new flat-rate pension system – introduced in 2016 – bears some comparison with how a citizen's income could work, though low income pensioners are still entitled to receive means-tested pensioner credit.

The fourth wave

Today, we are in a fourth wave, one that emerged following the 2008 Crash and has been gathering pace over the past few years. This latest surge in interest can be seen most powerfully in the trials currently underway in Finland, Canada and the Netherlands. Although these trials, which began in 2017, have their critics – and mostly fall short of being full UBI experiments – they have fuelled momentum behind the idea.

This new wave is being driven by a variety of factors. The first of these has been the disruptive impact of ongoing social and economic change, from de-industrialisation to austerity, all contributing to significant shifts in the nature of work. For a growing proportion of national workforces, job markets have become much more fragile, leading in many countries to a stagnation in living standards and a sharp rise in in-work poverty.

A second driver has been growing concern about the impact of the 'new machine age'. The likely impact of the robotic revolution – from 3D printing and algorithms to driverless cars and machine-driven journalism – is hotly debated. Several studies have predicted that a significant proportion of today's jobs could be automated over the next two decades.[8] Others accept that we are on the cusp of an IT revolution, but argue that the effect will be weaker than widely predicted.[9] The full scale of the impact is inevitably uncertain, and there are big questions about how companies will adopt these new technologies in practice. What is likely, however, is widespread and prolonged job upheaval at every level – just think of the impact of prolonged deindustrialisation on livelihoods – from manual work through to the professions, as complex decisions are made better and faster by machines. What is likely is an even more polarised workforce, with, in particular, middle-paid jobs replaced by poorly-paid ones.

Added to this, the current system of social security – originally designed for a very different post-war world – is poorly equipped to deal with the growing insecurity and polarisation of the 21st century. In the UK and elsewhere, it has become more heavily reliant on means testing and less on universalism. In recent times, there has been an increase in the level of conditionality, with the obligations imposed for receipt of benefits often operated in a punitive and intrusive way.

By cushioning citizens from today's great winds of change, a UBI would be an effective tool for tackling growing economic risk. With its built-in income guarantee, it would bring a more robust safety net in a much more precarious and fast-changing work environment and would lower the risk of poverty among those in work. It would boost the universal element of income support, reduce dependency on means testing and bring an end to policing and sanctioning.

Despite the risk of significant disruption, the robotic revolution may have an important upside – a potentially sizeable productivity dividend (although it is yet to appear) and thus potentially new social and economic opportunities.[10] But the risk is that such gains would be colonised by an elite of financiers and technologists leading to another hike in inequality along with a weakening of demand. In 1931, in *The Economic Possibilities for Our Grandchildren*, J.M. Keynes predicted that by 2030, the growth of productivity would have created a society sufficiently rich that most people would choose more leisure and less work. In the event, Keynes was right about technological progress, but wrong about leisure.

The new technological revolution opens up a possible route to the vision set out by Keynes. If the productivity boost from automation turns out to be as significant as some predict, and the fruits are harnessed for the benefit of all, there is the possibility of a fairer and less harassed society. But this vision can only be realised if any productivity gains are more equally shared, one of the great policy challenges of the future. One of the strengths of a UBI is its potential to help move to that vision, by ensuring redistribution from the winners of the tech revolution to the rest, and helping to realise the new potential for choice offered by the new technology. Indeed, a basic income is part of the answer to the growing search for models of 'inclusive growth' in which the gains from economic progress are shared by all and not colonised by capital.

However, a UBI is not just about finding a practical solution to the rise of precarity and accelerating automation. Indeed, one of its galvanising forces has been the way a UBI would transform the nature of choice. Central to a UBI is that it is non-prescriptive: it would offer people greater flexibility between work, leisure (and let's not confuse leisure with idleness), education and caring. It offers everyone greater freedom and autonomy, progressive changes with transformative potential.

Some might choose to work less or take longer breaks between jobs. Others would be incentivised to start businesses, perhaps strengthening the potential of the gig economy. Some might take time to retrain, while others might devote more time to leisure, personal care or community support. Such a boost to choice has the potential to produce more social value, if currently unrecognised, than some paid work. To make this explicit, it is time that the national accounts recognised the economic contribution of such activity.

Implicit to the idea is that all lifestyle choices would be equally valued. A UBI would value but not over-value work. A UBI would, for the first time, both acknowledge and provide financial support for the mass of unpaid work from childcare to voluntary help – disproportionately undertaken by women and of significant, but too often unacknowledged value. As a UBI is paid to individuals, the opening up of greater choice would be especially beneficial to women. By providing basic security, a UBI would also help boost labour's greatly depleted bargaining power with employers, offering more choice over what jobs to take, and opening up the possibility that employers would need to offer jobs, that in the phrase of Bertrand Russell, are 'not disagreeable'.[11]

The precise impact on work patterns and pay is unpredictable. A UBI would, over time, change behaviour, possibly significantly, and the results of the national pilots will provide important new evidence of these dynamic effects on employment, earnings, and working age poverty. The net effect, supported in part by evidence from earlier pilots, is more likely to promote than weaken the incentive to work, as well as acting as an inducement to earn more. Indeed, incentives would be stimulated by lowering dependency on means testing.

Of course, there is no single model of UBI on offer. Advocates come from very different perspectives and levels of ambition. Most supporters accept that a UBI is not a silver bullet that would solve all today's problems, but see it as a source of empowerment that could lead to better work for many, while taking the sting out of a much more precarious and insecure future. They view a UBI as aiming to tackle the greater risks of a weakened labour market, not to promote an end to work.

Some see UBI as a way to rejig the present tax and benefit system to make it more progressive and build a firmer floor. The libertarian right see it as a substitute for large parts of existing welfare systems. A small group advocate basic income as an essential element of a utopian 'post-capitalist', 'post-work' world, well beyond the Keynesian vision.[12] Another approach – which can be traced in particular to Thomas Paine and, in the 20th century, to the work of James Meade[13] – sees UBI as part of a package of progressive reforms that would aim to fund a generous scheme as part of a wider socialisation of the economy. In this model, UBI would take the form of a regular 'social dividend' – 'a people's stake' – paid from a collectively owned citizen's wealth fund formed at least in part from the better management of common assets. It is this approach that underpins the Alaskan social dividend.

Such an approach would be transformative and derives from the principle that a large part of modern physical and social wealth is inherited – 'gifts of society as well as nature' – and should be held in common with the benefits equally shared.[14]

Currently the only one of these models really on the political agenda is the first and, despite the recent surge in interest, the idea of a UBI remains highly controversial. Left and right supporters, for example, have very different visions. Left advocates view such a scheme as part of a strong state, as a way of securing a robust income floor, of tackling poverty and as a means of promoting equal citizenship. They are clear that a UBI must be seen as a supplement to the wider public provision of services and not as a substitute.

The libertarian right, however, mostly favour a basic income as an opportunity to sweep away other forms of social protection and some welfare institutions. In both Milton Friedman and Charles Murray's formulations, it was designed to replace the bulk of America's welfare programme, and allow market forces much freer rein.[15] The support coming from Silicon Valley enthusiasts, many of whom are driving the new gig economy and stand to gain substantially from the technological revolution, comes with a mix of motives. While some of these innovators see the idea as essential to create a fairer society, others favour it as a way of defusing potential opposition to the march of automation, or as a substitute for parts of the existing welfare structure. These contrasting positions are incompatible and it is inconceivable that a scheme could be devised that satisfied both sides.

But the idea of a UBI is also a 'Marmite issue' within the left. Opponents claim it is unaffordable and would undermine the work ethic, and are against the removal of conditions from the receipt of benefit. There is also concern about the shift in emphasis from the post-war principle of national insurance based on contributions and the sharing of risk, and how far 'a no strings attached' payment would gain a similar level of public buy-in. Left enthusiasts, on the other hand, claim that a modest scheme is affordable, that a UBI paid as a right would enhance freedom and promote greater social justice by the creation of a robust income floor, while conditionality is much less appropriate in an age of growing uncertainty. For them, it is a profoundly democratic and egalitarian concept, based on a recognition that all citizens have the right to some minimal claim on national income.

The contributions

All of these issues are covered in the chapters that follow. The chapters come from a diversity of contributors, offering a great range of views and insights from Canada, Uganda, Kenya and India as well as the UK, US and continental Europe. While most contributors favour some kind of UBI, though with differences of emphasis, and sometimes with questions, there are also a handful of voices making the case against.

Part I presents the multifaceted case for a UBI. Silicon Valley's Martin Ford sees a UBI as the only 'viable solution' to the impact of artificial intelligence. Eduardo Rodriguez-Montemayor, at Paris-based INSEAD, sets out the 'empowerment' arguments. Chris Oesteriech, founder of America's 'Wicked Problems Collaborative', shows how a UBI would provide 'financial padding for future downturns'.

Sharing his own experience of building a career, the musician and composer Brian Eno argues that a basic income would help to nurture and support creativity. For musician Toby Deller, a basic income would help 'keep music alive'. Ursula Barry from Dublin argues that as long as it is accompanied by other policies that challenge gender inequality, a basic income could promote greater economic independence for women. Vanessa Olorenshaw, a founding member of the Women's Equality Party, shows how a basic income would address the issue of unwaged work done by women in the home and the community. Karl Widerquist, co-founder of the US Basic Income Guarantee Network, makes a powerful personal statement about the merits of the idea, while Labour peer Ruth Lister CBE, a leading UK authority on social security, explains why she has finally 'come off the fence'.

Part II presents the arguments from a range of leading campaigning organisations and supporting politicians, who believe that a basic income is essential in building a bridge to the future with a new emphasis on empowerment, innovation and fairness. As Anthony Painter from the Royal Society of Arts puts it, 'We are trying to build tomorrow's society with the politics of today'. On this futuristic theme, Roope Mokka and

Katariina Rantanen from the independent think-tank Demos Helsinki argue that it offers citizens a new capacity 'to participate actively in society'. The contribution from Canada's *The Leap Manifesto* ('a roadmap for a better future') argues that a UBI offers the prospect of greater 'democratic control of resources and productive assets'. Brenton Caffin from UK innovation think-tank Nesta suggests that a UBI has the power to 'unlock a new economic and innovation revolution'.

Olivia Hanks from the online progressive publication Norwich Radical proposes that because most material wealth belongs to society as a whole, a UBI is needed to ensure such wealth is more fairly distributed. The political case is made by Jonathan Bartley and Caroline Lucas MP, joint leaders of the UK Green Party, the Labour MP Jonathan Reynolds and Uffe Elbæk, leader of Denmark's Alternativet Party.

Part III brings some counter-views. Francine Mestrum, chairwoman of the Global Social Justice network, argues that it would be better to strengthen existing systems of social protection. Ian Gough of the London School of Economics fears the UBI debate will 'divert' attention from wider progressive goals while citizen participation advocate, Peter Beresford, raises important questions about the top down nature of UBI. Ed Whitfield, co-founder of the American Fund for Democratic Communities, argues that basic income is not transformative enough and public policy academic Anke Hassel claims that a UBI is merely a 'dead end'.

Part IV offers a variety of perspectives on the politics of a basic income and how it could be made to happen. Belgian philosopher and longstanding advocate of a UBI, Philippe Van Parijs, argues that it is time that social democrats moved on from post-war models of social assistance to embrace this new approach. Malcolm Torry, director of the Citizen's Basic Income Trust, examines the recent history of the debate in the UK, while Louise Haagh, co-chair of BIEN, argues it should be seen as a way to 're-democratise the state'.

With the Indian government declaring it is time for a 'serious deliberation' on a national UBI,[16] Sarath Davala and Soumya

Kapoor Mehta discuss the positive outcomes from the 2009–13 Indian pilot. Annie Miller, co-founder of the Citizen's Basic Income Network Scotland, looks at the options facing the three councils – Glasgow, Fife and North Ayrshire – that have declared an initial interest in hosting a pilot. Philosophy academic Matt Zwolinski puts the libertarian case and proposes a two-tier model, part universal, part means tested. Andrew Harrop, General Secretary of the Fabian Society, and economists Stewart Lansley and Howard Reed offer two different perspectives on how it could be made to work in practice.

Part V looks at a number of countries at the forefront of the action, including the state of play with the various trials under way or being planned. Otto Lehto, founder of BIEN Finland, discusses the Finnish trial, the first of the contemporary pilots, launched in January 2017. Campaigners Roderick Benns and Jenna van Draanen examine the latest on the Canadian trials, while Alexander de Roo, co-founder of BIEN in 1986, outlines the complex background to the Dutch pilots launched in late 2017.

As well as these state sponsored and funded trials, there are contributions from four of the smaller pilots financed by charities and individuals: Y Combinator's experiment in basic income in Oakland, California; the crowd-funded, small-scale project in Uganda, run by the Belgium charity, Eight; the Kenyan trial run by charity GiveDirectly and the small-scale project in Brazil launched in 2008 by the ReCivitas Institute. Finally, Part VI looks at 'the way forward'.

Despite the recent surge in interest, the debate has been mostly confined to a relatively narrow circle, with articles and books appealing mostly to academics and practitioners with an existing interest in the idea. In planning this book, our aim has been to feature a wide range of shortish pieces, offering an array of views – spanning activists, researchers, writers and some doubters – from across the world. By hearing of views and developments, past and present, across such a diversity of societies and nations, our hope is that the book will appeal more widely, and thereby help to spread the debate, a vital step if the idea is to become a reality.

PART I:
THE CASE FOR

1

As artificial intelligence and robotics advance, a basic income may be the only viable solution

Martin Ford, USA

'The goal should be to leverage the power of artificial intelligence and robotics for the benefit of society.'

Recent progress in artificial intelligence and robotics suggests that we are likely to see astonishing advances over the course of the coming decades. These innovations will make the production of goods and services of all kinds more efficient and affordable and are sure to have enormous benefits for all of humanity.

There is, however, a dark side to this progress: a great many workers will likely face displacement by machines. A large percentage of jobs are, on some level, essentially routine and repetitive in nature. As machine learning and robotics technologies advance, a large fraction of these job types will be at risk of being automated.

This concern is not dependent on far-fetched science fiction-level technology: rather, it is based on a simple extrapolation of the expert systems and sophisticated algorithms that can currently land jet airplanes, trade autonomously on Wall Street, or – as recently demonstrated by Google's DeepMind technology – beat nearly any human being at the ancient game of 'Go'. As technology progresses, these systems will begin to match or exceed the capability of human workers in many routine jobs – and this includes a lot of workers with college degrees or other significant training. Many workers will also be increasingly threatened by the continuing trend toward self-service technologies that push tasks onto consumers.

Those who are sceptical that advancing technology might create significant unemployment are likely to cite one of the most extreme historical examples of technologically induced job losses: the mechanisation of agriculture. In the late 1800s, about 75% of workers in the United States were employed in agriculture. Today, the number is around 2%. Advancing technology irreversibly eliminated millions of jobs.

When agriculture mechanised, we did not end up with long-term structural unemployment. Workers were eventually absorbed by other industries, and over the long term, average wages and overall prosperity increased dramatically. The historical experience with agriculture is, in fact, an excellent illustration of the so-called 'Luddite fallacy'. This idea, generally accepted by economists – if far from controversy free, suggests that technological progress will never lead to broad-based, long-term unemployment. The reasoning behind the Luddite fallacy goes roughly like this: As labour-saving technologies improve, some workers lose their jobs in the short run, but production also becomes more efficient. That leads to lower prices for the goods and services produced, and that, in turn, leaves consumers with more money to spend on other things. When they do so, demand increases across nearly all industries–and that means more jobs. That seems to be exactly what happened with agriculture: food prices fell as efficiency increased, and then consumers went out and spent their extra money elsewhere, driving increased employment in the manufacturing and service sectors.

The question we face now is whether or not that same scenario is likely to play out again.[1] The problem is that this time we are not talking about a single industry being automated: artificial intelligence (AI) and robotics are general purpose technologies and will penetrate across the board. When agriculture mechanised, there were clearly other labour-intensive sectors capable of absorbing the workers. There's little evidence to suggest that's going to be the case this time around.

It seems likely that, as automation penetrates nearly everywhere, and nearly all kinds of routine predictable work disappears, there must come a 'tipping point,' beyond which the overall economy is simply not labour intensive enough to continue absorbing workers who lose their jobs due to automation (or globalisation). Beyond this point, businesses will be able to ramp up production primarily by employing machines and software – and structural unemployment then becomes inevitable.

If we reach that point, then we will also face a serious problem with consumer demand. If automation is relentless, then the basic mechanism that gets purchasing power into the hands of consumers begins to break down. That creates the potential for an economic scenario where there are too few viable consumers to drive economic growth and prosperity. Economies would then face the risk of stagnation or even a deflationary spiral.

Over the course of the coming decades, nations throughout the world will face the challenge of adapting to this new reality. The goal should be to leverage the power of artificial intelligence and robotics for the benefit of society, while finding a way to mitigate the potential impact on employment, economic security and consumer confidence. Because artificial intelligence is proving adept at climbing the skills ladder – tasks performed by highly educated workers like journalists, lawyers and radiologists are already being impacted – simply relying on the traditional policy of ever more training and education for affected workers is unlikely to be a sustainable solution.

Instead, we will have to find a way to restructure our economic system, and that will likely involve decoupling income from traditional jobs. Some form of guaranteed income or universal basic income (UBI) is the most viable way to achieve this. The idea is that we would provide everyone with at least a minimal unconditional income that would provide basic economic security as well as the means to participate in the economy as a consumer.

As artificial intelligence and robotics advance, a basic income may be the only viable solution

Because implementing a UBI is sure to represent a staggering political challenge, it is important to be pragmatic. In my books, *Rise of the Robots* (2015) and *The Lights in the Tunnel* (2009), I suggested two ways that an absolutely 'universal' and 'unconditional' basic income scheme might be modified to make it more effective, affordable and politically palatable.

First, basic incentives could be incorporated. Most important would be an incentive to pursue further education. Those who complete higher levels of education should receive higher basic incomes. In the absence of this, non-academically inclined students might be presented with a perverse incentive to drop out of school, knowing that they would, in any case, be eligible for the basic income. Education is an important public good, and a well-educated population provides benefits to society. Any basic income scheme should be designed to ensure that citizens continue to experience direct, personal gain from remaining in school. Such incentives might also be extended to other areas, such as meaningful contributions to communities or to humanistic or artistic endeavours.

Secondly, one of the most important tenets of a UBI is that the income is not means tested. Everyone receives the income unconditionally. This ensures that there is no disincentive to work or engage in entrepreneurial activity that will result in a higher overall income level. In theory, it should also help to galvanise political support. This approach is, however, much more costly than a guaranteed minimum income that is phased out as other income increases. I think there is middle ground that could reduce the overall cost of a UBI while making it more politically feasible: the income could be means tested against 'passive' income (pensions, social security, rents and royalties, investment income) but not against 'active' income (wages, income from an actively managed small business, etc.). This would preserve the incentive to work or start a business, while reducing the cost of the programme. It would also improve the political optics by limiting the eligibility of those who already enjoy adequate guaranteed incomes from other sources.

As artificial intelligence and robotics advance, a basic income may be the only viable solution

While UBI purists will likely voice many objections to these ideas, it seems likely that compromises will be required if a basic income is ever to become politically viable. The first step should be to initiate some pilot programmes to test various basic income schemes. These experiments would provide data to be used to craft an eventual programme that could be scaled out at national levels. We should begin as soon as possible. Information technology continues to advance exponentially, and the impact on the job market could well materialise long before we are prepared for it.

As artificial intelligence and robotics advance, a basic income may be the only viable solution

2

Could a universal basic income become the basis for working better in a fast-changing world?

Eduardo Rodriguez-Montemayor, INSEAD, France

'UBI can help achieve the adaptability and flexibility required by the 21st century economy. People will take on the opportunities brought by technology as long as they can afford to leave jobs, take risks and get the relevant training.'

When a London-based start-up in the domain of financial information began using a robo-writer (called Quill) to produce automated reports, its own employees were shocked. The result was so indistinguishable from the one produced by human analysts that many people risk losing their jobs.

If analysts are worried about potentially being replaced by machines, just imagine the apprehension faced by workers doing more manual or routine jobs.

In an article explaining why a universal basic income (UBI) could be a good idea, I framed the discussion precisely in this context of rapid technological change.[2] The fear is that many jobs will be replaced by machines – thus creating 'technological unemployment'. The idea of UBI is thus gaining momentum as a way of better sharing the dividends of technology-driven economic growth.

A UBI is an unconditional payment granted to every individual as a right of citizenship. People may then work to earn their regular wage on top of that. Although the idea of UBI has been around for centuries, it has never taken off despite pilots in some countries. A main concern is the cost to public coffers. *The Economist* magazine suggests that we should not bother with the 'exorbitant' cost UBI would represent given that a main reason for its introduction, which is widespread technological unemployment, is not a reality yet – and it may never arrive.[3]

The specialists of the weekly have a point. Many economists still believe that the automation of some jobs will be offset by the creation of new jobs, just as has happened in previous industrial revolutions (see Chapter 1). But this is why UBI makes sense. Although we are not at all near the apocalypse of work, we are working differently. People no longer have the linear career paths of the 20th century, with a single long-term employer. Contingent and project-based work are on the rise. Industries and business models are constantly changing, and so too are the types of jobs available, so people will have to adapt and move to the new jobs being created. Therefore, new institutions and policies are needed.

The empowerment effect: UBI would make people flourish

UBI can help achieve the adaptability and flexibility required by the 21st century economy. People will take on the opportunities brought by technology as long as they can afford to leave jobs, take risks and get the relevant training. The process of upskilling and moving to new jobs takes time and money and a basic income could become the ally to make it possible. In this way, UBI would help make people work more and also work better.

This is a view that is opposite to the widely made criticism that people will not bother to work any more while receiving 'free' cash. But this critique is wrong. First, *UBI could lead people to work more*. The criticism that under UBI people will just not bother to work anymore is similar to criticisms levelled at unemployment insurance. But unemployment and other welfare benefits are contingent on not working or on being poor. Because a universal income is conferred on everyone, it avoids the issue that some people have an incentive to work less in order to meet the conditions for being eligible, and thus avoids the welfare traps of means-tested or conditional programmes.

Secondly, by adapting to the fast-changing world, acquiring the right skills and, more importantly, having the incentives to go the extra mile, *UBI could lead people to work better*. Because of this, under a UBI, the economy would become more productive by facilitating the efficient reallocation of talent. Moreover, if it is the case that people work more and adapt, then UBI does not have to be out of reach financially.

This potential empowerment effect suggests that UBI would also help people fulfil their potential and become more productive. In addition, some workers would regain bargaining power by being more able to leave jobs that offer unacceptable working conditions. The empowerment created by all these potential benefits is what Philippe Van Parijs calls 'real freedom for all'.[4]

We do not yet have much evidence to confirm the empowerment effect. There have been few UBI pilots, and the impact of the current and planned pilots (see Part V) will not be known for some while. But studies have shown that certain types of cash transfers can have positive effects, such as increasing the willingness to bear risk.[5] Also, studies have not found that cash transfers make people stop working,[6] as can be the case with means-tested programmes.[7] The various new pilots around the world will provide further evidence on these effects.

The numbers: the programme can be affordable

It is also important to clarify some confusions about a UBI's affordability: a UBI would not be as costly as it seems. Martin Sandbu of the *Financial Times* has examined the affordability of such a programme for the UK and has explained some confusions arising when discussing the fiscal consequences of UBI in different countries.

One confusion has to do with how much countries actually spend on social transfers in existing protection systems. This confusion leads to overestimations of the extra tax money needed to run a UBI. According to calculations by *The Economist*, a UBI roughly equal to one-third of average income per head would require a tax take in Britain that is more than 20 percentage points larger.[8] But as Sandbu writes, 'this is misleading because the share of the government's tax take and redistributive spending in the economy does not include tax exemptions and allowances, where the state selectively refrains from imposing normal taxes.'[9] Such 'tax expenditures' – the money not raised – would represent additional income if replaced by UBI. In the UK in 2017, for example, the first £11,500 is exempt from income tax. This exemption costs around £100 billion in tax revenue annually.

By converting tax allowances into a cash payment, UBI would eliminate such hidden expenditures. As explained by Sandbu, it is better to think of UBI as a tax policy, not a welfare spending policy.[10]

Different value systems and looking ahead

In addition to these economic arguments, there is also a social justice case for UBI. This is based on the notion of shared ownership of a nation's wealth. Wealth creation is driven by individual efforts, of course, but also by a form of collective intelligence reflected in a country's institutions and social heritage from past efforts.[11]

Nevertheless, different countries have different value systems and giving people money without any work conditions may be difficult to digest politically in some countries. UBI might succeed in Finland but not in, say, Hong Kong. Winning the case for UBI will therefore require the engagement of policy makers, corporations and academics on the merits of such a programme in the context of different value systems. Universal basic education was revolutionary when it was introduced in the early 20th century. But it was needed in the context of the industrial age. Production and work practices had changed and a mechanism for creating the skills required by the economy was urgent.

Today, we are also witnessing a transformation in the world of work from new technologies, globalisation and demographic change. This time, it is the adaptability of people that is urgent. Our welfare systems are more than a century old and responded to the first waves of industrialisation (those of mechanisation, mass production and computerisation). Today the 4th industrial revolution of smart, data-driven production is changing the context of work once again.[12]

Despite its economic and social justice merits, UBI would not be a panacea for all our economic challenges. Inequality, for example, would continue growing if the top of the pyramid were able to reap disproportionate benefits from technology. UBI can help ensure a basic standard of living for large segments of society but relative deprivation (more relevant than absolute deprivation) would still persist. Even if technology leads to more growth, discontent and frustration are partly relativistic, and driven not just by a sense of absolute stagnation. Ensuring that all individuals retain a basic claim on some minimal share of national prosperity, rather than a minimal amount of money as in UBI, becomes the deeper policy question.

I want to hear more about the link between UBI and inequalities because the largely intangible nature of inter-generational advantages that hinder social mobility raises doubts about how far taxation and redistribution can alleviate inequality. UBI is a way to lessen workers' pain as they move from declining industries and skillsets to rising ones. Yet, putting a little money in everyone's pockets does not raise the slumping hopes of the people that are falling behind. Even with a UBI that could finance access to some training and other opportunities, underprivileged people may not see, let alone seize, the slender opportunities available to them. The increasing divergence of aspirations between the winners and losers of a fast-changing economy may perpetuate inequalities across generations – in the extent to which people in poorer backgrounds get locked into low-skill occupations as their parents did.

I am enthusiastic about scaling up discussions about UBI. I believe in the empowerment argument. But I want to hear more. Implementing UBI would require higher tax rates on higher earners than most countries levy today, thereby contributing to the wider goal of reducing inequality. But a key question remains as to how to achieve a more redistributive system without having talented people flee to countries with lower taxes.[13]

I would also like to hear more about different ways of financing UBI (for example, by creating social wealth funds or citizens' trusts[14]) and about how such a programme would compare with other options for encouraging upskilling and job mobility such as the flexicurity approach adopted in Denmark (see Chapter 17). Such discussions will need a detailed vision of the implementation of UBI in different country contexts and value systems, including which welfare programmes would be eliminated – without falling into what Amartya Sen has called (in reference to India) the 'abdication of responsibility' by neglecting other policy areas such as education.[15]

As a final reflection, universality means that a basic income would be received as a right of citizenship. But my colleague at INSEAD, Paul Evans, drew my attention to the fact that the Danes base their flexicurity approach on the premise that citizens not only have rights but also obligations. This made me think: should UBI then be available for everyone that meets her or his obligations as citizens, for instance, to all people that go out and vote? This would be a great boost for 'l'esprit de civisme'. I want to hear more. The discussion just begins.

3

An economic shock absorber

Chris Oestereich, USA

'Basic incomes would provide a bit of financial padding for future downturns ... This would have the additional benefit of tempering any loss of spending and thereby reducing the negative demand shock of the downturn.'

The idea of the job as we've long known it is slowly unravelling. Things that we've been taught to expect – full-time employment, training, and opportunities for promotion – are all eroding.[16] What sort of world will we have if these trends continue? And how long could it remain stable?

While the global middle class (in emerging nations) has experienced gains in recent years, those at the top of the economic heap are still pulling away from the pack. And the gains experienced by the former group look vulnerable as developing nations around the world cue up to vie for limited opportunities.[17] In general, the 'have nots' are less likely to be moving in a direction of safety, security, and self-actualisation, and more likely to be scrambling to survive in ever more precarious circumstances.

The widely shared prosperity of the mid-20th century increasingly appears to have been an historical anomaly. Throughout the middle of the 20th century, American workers enjoyed rising wages that roughly tracked rising productivity.

Since then, wage levels have largely stagnated, while CEO pay has boomed.

As the US unemployment level subsides, there's hope that wages will finally head in a better direction, and the 2016 US Census Report gave us surprisingly good news to that end. From 2014 to 2015, median household income rose 5.2% (the first such increase since the Great Recession), the number of full-time, year-round workers increased by 2.4 million, and the number of people living below the poverty line dropped by 3.5 million.[18] But another recent study suggests that half a billion jobs will be needed 'as soon as 2020' to eliminate the global glut of unemployment, while also providing those necessitated by population growth.[19] (Don't worry. We'll figure out how to make them into good jobs later.) So while forces inside the US economy may favour local workers, others on the outside will continue to provide a countervailing force.

The income gains that the census uncovered are being heralded by some as a sign that we're finally headed for brighter days. If this trend continues, then my argument might end up well off the mark. But history appears to be on my side. Since the Great Depression era, the period between recessions has been getting steadily shorter.

Moving beyond the boom-and-bust cycles that define our economy will require an upgrade to the economic operating system that hasn't yet occurred. As a result, our 'fortunes' continue to float on an economic bubble that will eventually pop. So, it's time to consider what we might do to change the system and, to start, we need to question our fundamental assumptions about how to organise the economy and society in general.

The belief that the profit motive is the optimal incentive for driving progress is often treated as a given. But although we know there are people who are driven by the profit motive, and maybe we all are to some degree, there are plenty of other factors driving human behaviour. Why should we believe that one takes complete precedence over the rest when we

An economic shock absorber

know that some of us are also pulled by things like the need to foster a sense of community, the desire to support family and friends, or even a compulsion to work on the wicked problems faced by humanity?[20] Each of us has a mix of forces pulling us in different directions. At best, the profit motive is an oversimplification. At worst, it's a destructive force without equal.

Regardless of the reality of our motivations, our economic system remains centered on the profit motive. If I want a roof over my head, and something to eat, I better do something that affords me the necessary income. If I want to spend all of my time helping others, but no one is willing to pay me enough to cover my needs, I'd better have deep enough pockets to live off. But what if we had a different system, one in which our primary needs were taken care of? What might that system look like? A universal basic income is one possible answer.

Can it help?

Given a monthly payment that set a moderate income floor, but didn't remove the support provided by other safety net programmes (things like Medicare, SNAP, and WIC in the United States), the question about universal basic incomes is not whether they would help those who are struggling to make ends meet (they would), but whether they might create any undesirable macroeconomic effects like runaway inflation.

US economist Brad DeLong recently offered a checklist that might serve as a useful starting place. The list, which aimed to enumerate the things 'any rightly arranged society has to successfully do,' included: setting up frameworks for the (1) production and (2) distribution of stuff, (3) creating a very dense reciprocal network of interdependencies to ensure that we are all one society, and doing so in such a way that (4) people do not see themselves, are not seen as, and are not either saps or moochers.[21]

1. The production of stuff is already occurring, and although it will continue to evolve, it seems unlikely that this would suddenly unwind with the introduction of a basic income. Some people might choose to work less, but those who were struggling would be able to consume more. Prior experiments, like the one run in Canada during the 1970s, have not uncovered problems along these lines.[22] That said, we probably need to try larger experiments, and do a better job of studying them, to get a handle on potential macroeconomic impacts.

2. The distribution of stuff is largely limited by our collective ability to consume, which is limited by our individual ability to pay. Willingness, desire, and even necessity do not put food on the table. A universal basic income would help remove the barriers that prevent people from attaining basic necessities.

3. Whether UBI will help us strengthen our ties seems less straightforward. I'm sure some will look at it as a handout, and therefore a detractor from social cohesion. Others will likely see it as a path to stronger bonds through the reduction of precarity, and the increased opportunity for connection through the reduced necessity for seeking and performing paid work. Volunteering is much easier when you are not working two (or more) jobs just to avoid the harsh penalties of coming up short when the rent is due.

4. Finally, there is the question of reciprocity. The answer to this will be a matter of public perception. Will a basic income be viewed as a handout or as a fair deal that helps facilitate an orderly society? Many will seek to demonize such a programme, but given a fair shake, solidarity can - and likely will - triumph.

Is it a perfect cure-all?

Universal basic income appears to have a lot to offer in improving the way that society functions, but we shouldn't expect it to fix our every economic woe. In proposing an idea that would be a significant departure from the way our economy currently functions, it's incumbent on agitators to be honest about what

An economic shock absorber

they believe the changes could and could not achieve, as well as about any potential downsides those changes might foster.

With that in mind, I believe that UBI would help deliver more broadly just economic outcomes, in which suffering due to financial shortcomings could be greatly reduced. But while greatly curtailing poverty, I don't think basic incomes should be expected to eliminate the condition. And plenty of other potential pitfalls may lie waiting in the road ahead. Thinking about what problems might lurk, and designing experiments with those possibilities in mind, should help us arrive at a workable starting point. A few potential obstacles I see are (1) the likelihood of rent seeking, (2) the curtailment of welfare programmes, and (3) the financialisation of basic incomes.

1. The economy is already rife with rent seeking; the pursuit of economic gain without reciprocation. Imagine what those who already pursue such 'opportunities' might try when they learn that everyone will start receiving regularly scheduled checks. What would cartoonishly rapacious capitalists like Turing Pharmaceuticals[23] and the EpiPen's maker Mylan,[24] and all the profiteers who keep their inequitable dealings under the radar do in those circumstances? And if prices were to rise, whether due to the force of rising demand or the unnatural machinations of the aforementioned grasping entities, is there a chance we could tip the economy into runaway inflation? Failing an exorbitant basic income – a seemingly implausible outcome – I think it's highly unlikely to occur. But again this is the point of thorough, thoughtful experimentation.

2. Many advocates see it as a path to cost savings in welfare. Their goal is to reduce the overall expenditure by replacing means-tested benefits (thereby removing the associated administrative costs) with basic incomes. The danger in this is that the recipient who gains a basic income, but loses other benefits, could easily end up worse off overall. Consolidating programmes can yield gains in efficiency, but this should not come at the cost of suffering.

An economic shock absorber

3. Finally, basic incomes will act as annuities – steady streams of income that can be counted on in timing and amount. Financial products featuring lump sum payments (much like those offered with lottery jackpots) could be used to rob people of what's meant to be their monthly living allowance, while others might try to capture this income for the repayment of debts. Given Wall Street's (and the City's) past financialization efforts, we can expect these to be difficult to ward off. We've been through enough to know that if we leave a fresh pie on the window sill, it won't be long before someone absconds with it. Without active mobilisation to anticipate and head off such attempts, such programmes could be expected to proliferate, so I would aim for an explicit denial of any such instruments.

A cushion for future shocks

Recessions tend to hit people unevenly. Some squeeze through relatively unaffected. Some muddle through when they might otherwise move on to better opportunities. Some lose their jobs, settling for lower-paying ones or getting by thanks to social safety nets. Some fall through the cracks.

Basic incomes would provide a bit of financial padding for future downturns. Those who lose their work income would still have something coming in each month. This would have the additional benefit of tempering any loss of spending and thereby reducing the negative demand shock of the downturn.

Although the Great Recession formally ended seven years ago, recovery in the United States has been fairly weak. Simmering economic, political, and social issues remain, bearing the ever-present possibility of another downturn. Every tremor reminds us of the economic fault line under Wall Street, and many people are in far more precarious circumstances than they were at the end of the last bull market.

Given these risks, it is incumbent upon those who are aware of the need to demand change while it can still be done in a thoughtful, orderly fashion, thus reducing the unnecessary

An economic shock absorber

suffering that's happening now, while trying to head off the turmoil that waits ahead. Universal basic incomes appear to be an opportunity to move humanity in a more just direction. I hope you'll agree, and that you'll lend your voice to the growing chorus that's advocating for this change.

An economic shock absorber

4

Questioning the 'natural order'

Brian Eno, UK

'Basic income is a radical notion. It seems to question the "natural order" of things.'

Most of the great social innovations that humans have achieved must have looked ridiculously idealistic until they actually happened. Imagine what a medieval peasant would have thought of the idea that she might be given a vote, a say in how the rulers ruled her? Wouldn't her reaction have been one of pure scepticism: 'What's the catch? Why are they doing it?' And, if you'd managed to convince her that there wasn't a catch, wouldn't it have required a huge leap of imagination to envisage a world where anything like a Parliamentary democracy could exist, with would-be rulers having to compete peacefully with each other to capture public support, liable to be voted out if they failed to satisfy that public? It would have seemed like pure idealistic fantasy. The same would be true of the abolition of slavery, voting rights for women, the National Health Service, and the abolition of child labour: all pie-in-the-sky until they happened.

Now all of those ideas seem to us self-evident. We take them for granted: a world without any one of them would look like a bleaker, more primitive place.

Basic income is a radical notion. It seems to question the 'natural order' of things. But the natural order is just what we've become used to. Society is a construction of beliefs in which we all take part – if even simply by not questioning them. The natural order once held, with great certainty, that *of course* children should work, that *of course* black people were incapable of the finer human feelings that Northern Europeans shared, that *of course* women were not intellectual beings capable of forming an opinion about politics. Basic income calls into question another fundamental premise of Western civilisation. We've all grown up with the idea that our identities are centred in our role as workers, and *of course* to be without a job is both socially irresponsible and morally shameful. We're not pulling our weight ... we're 'burdens on society'.

But are all the people who don't work *now* – and there are many – really burdens on society? Think of the women (and men) who'd prefer not to work but instead spend time bringing up their children. Is that a burden or a contribution? How about the several million Britons who spend a lot of their time looking after somebody else – somebody old or disabled. Are they burdens? And what about all the people who work for almost nothing anyway, doing something they believe in – like running a playgroup or a youth club or helping out at a local hospice or manning voting booths or helping kids across busy roads?

Not having to work a job doesn't mean you become useless: it means you're more free to decide what to do with your time. I'm certain that would mean a big upsurge in the number of people finding themselves able to do a lot of extremely useful things – socially useful things – that they simply couldn't have done before. The naysayers maintain that basic income would produce a nation of couch potatoes. Though it's probably true that there'd be a brief renaissance for daytime TV, I think there'd be a far greater – and longer lasting – renaissance in social action and community work. People like belonging to communities, enjoy contributing to them. It doesn't feel like work when it's what you want to do.

The difficulty that those of us who support basic income face is made clear by the failure of the Swiss referendum in 2016. The 'anti' campaign in Switzerland played on the issues of 'dignity of work' (as though we wouldn't be able to find dignity in any other way); and it played on the idea of 'freeloading' – a potent message in a fundamentally Calvinist society – by giving the impression that the people who were still 'working' would be supporting all those lazy sods who weren't. It was presented, and still is being presented, as a zero-sum game, where what one person gains another pays for. On that assumption, if some people stopped working, others would have to work more (or pay more taxes) to support them.

But it isn't like that: it isn't a zero-sum game. That assumption only makes sense if you think that all those people who decided not to work a normal job would not be doing anything productive at all – that they'd just sit at home eating cupcakes and watching TV. Believe it or not, most people wouldn't list that as their favourite occupation. A lot of them end up doing it because there's nothing more meaningful for them to do. But imagine a time when there was a lot to do, a lot to get involved in. Imagine your friend down the road decides to start a cooking club, or a singing group, or a political discussion group; or another friend now has the time to start a small business and needs a hand; or your church hall needs a paintjob and you've got the time on your hands. How long would you carry on watching Jeremy Kyle?

Since many of these things wouldn't involve the exchange of money, they pose a quandary for those many economists who assume that what you can't count, doesn't count. If there's no money involved in an activity, there's no quantifiable contribution to GNP: so the activity is economically invisible. But who would doubt that those activities make a huge difference to community life? And isn't that the fundamental objective? We all know that strong, richly connected communities have lower rates of crime and better health outcomes; that they look after their members better; that children benefit from the increased safety and breadth of inputs; that schools work better; that things get looked after instead of being allowed to fall apart.

So we have two sets of people to convince: the working people who have pinned their identity and their pride on having a job, and the economists for whom non-waged activity is invisible.

Perhaps we can placate both of them by saying 'Nobody *has* to stop working!' Of course you don't – but the difference would be that now you could work at something you really wanted to do, without the salary being the primary consideration. And if salary still was your primary consideration – if you really wanted to make money above all else – then you're welcome to go ahead and do that kind of job. There's good reason to suppose that salaries would rise for the less pleasant or more demanding jobs – and why shouldn't they? We underpay for them at the moment – because we know there's a pool of wage slaves who *have* to do them, or because we know there are people – like nurses and teachers – who feel a commitment to them.

Nothing upsets me more than waste, and no waste upsets me more than that of human potential and creativity. Look at children and their ceaseless curiosity and inventiveness ... and then at all the adults struggling on in dull and pointless jobs in order to pay the rent and have enough to eat. It makes me wonder that we can't arrange things better than this, can't think of ways to rethink our societies so that the enormous wellspring of human creativity so evident in childhood can be carried through routinely into adulthood.

Creativity takes time and stamina – and those are luxuries for many working people. Certainly my own trajectory in life was largely determined by the availability of National Assistance money for the few months after I left Art College. I came from a not-well-off family and without that financial support from the state I couldn't have held out long enough to help develop the band that became Roxy Music, and the whole career that followed. On a purely economic assessment the less-than-£400 the state invested in allowing me some time to find my feet has been rewarded many thousands of times by my tax contributions. If I had been forced into a job during that time I almost certainly wouldn't have had a career in music.

Basic income is a chance to reduce the urgency of sheer survival and liberate the potential of minds and imaginations. Imagination is our great gift as a species, but it isn't something that only a few people have: it's part of everyone's basic equipment.

When we look at children what we delight in is exactly that: their freedom, their love of play and experiment, their imagination. And then we send them to schools which, whatever their good intentions, are forced to be dedicated primarily to moulding them into a few simple niches – because occupying one of those niches is what you have to do to survive. Although a lot of people manage to break out of the pattern, a far greater number don't, and their natural creativity is gradually stifled. And that's a tragic waste.

Civilisation faces a vast array of challenges. To deal with them we need as many imaginations in play as we can mobilise. Basic income can help liberate those imaginations.

5

To keep music alive

Toby Deller, UK

'... for the creative artist, the true burden is not that they must work, but that they are prevented from working, at their art.'

It's a familiar image of classical musicians: a stage full of women and men in evening wear playing some symphony or other to an audience in a smart concert hall. But these figures in their penguin suits are really just the tip of a musical iceberg. Not only are classical musicians these days increasingly likely to be found in more relaxed clothing but they are much more likely to be found working on a much smaller and less obviously glamorous scale.

It is only a very small proportion of those training as classical musicians who end up with actual salaried work as performers (although contracts are such that even membership of a top orchestra does not necessarily come with a guaranteed annual salary). Orchestras are one of the very few employers of musicians; military bands are another, although that job comes with a variety of strings attached. Given the number of orchestras operating at that level in the UK, that amounts to around 1,500 positions in total - that's for all instruments - with hundreds of applicants for vacancies when they do come up. That's in a country whose seven main senior music colleges have, roughly, between 500 and 750 students on degree courses at any one time.

So, inevitably, musicians are likely to have to look outside performing to make their living. Often this will be in associated areas, principally teaching. While these are worthwhile and rewarding in themselves, they are likely to make it harder to take on freelance performing work when it does come along – freelance work of such a nature that it has to be carried out at given times and can't simply fit round other commitments – and still leaves the challenge of carving out enough opportunity to develop and promote one's own projects as well as keeping up proficiency on one's instrument. As many find, it's all too easy to sacrifice private practice under pressure of time, something you wouldn't expect a professional sportsperson to forego.

You may say that a similar situation holds for any artist, actor or indeed athlete, and that there's nothing special about classical musicians in this respect. And of course, that is essentially true. But the point here is that classical musicians (of whom I am one, being a freelance viola player) are part of a wide community that would benefit from the introduction of a universal basic income. In other words, the number and diversity of people who would benefit makes the universal basic income an even more compelling idea.

Put simply, a regular stipend along the lines of a universal basic income would give musicians the opportunity to devote more of their time to their creative work. But there are other potential benefits too. For example, it would give them an incentive to move away from the major cities, where the majority of work is to be found but where the cost of living can be challenging, to more affordable areas where it may be harder to pick up freelance work but where there is more scope to develop their own projects. That in turn has a social benefit for those areas that may currently be under-served relative to metropolitan areas.

Indeed, by alleviating the pressure on cost overheads it would be an encouragement to be creative with those projects in the first place. And as we move further into an age where recorded music becomes less and less lucrative as a source of a living for

To keep music alive

jobbing musicians (as the expectation grows that recorded music should be available free, or at least cheaply) but is not replaced by an alternative, an automatic income entitlement offers a potential means of compensation. A universal basic income could, with the proper agreements, turn into a de facto licensing system whereby the whole of society pays for the right of every individual to access the music they wish.

That, however, is probably for the future. In the meantime, it is the very universality of the universal basic income that means it cannot be seen either as additional money for privileged people who don't need it (one of the key arguments against the way state funding of the arts is seen to operate), or as free money for idle people who don't deserve it (because it is an investment in creativity, not stagnation). No longer would musicians and their fellow artists need to feel defensive about their status against the classic 'get a proper job'. After all, for the creative artist, the true burden is not that they must work, but that they are prevented from working, at their art.

To keep music alive

6

Feminist reflections on basic income

Ursula Barry, Ireland

'Basic income in itself may not be able to challenge the gender division of labour. However, it can bring about one critical condition necessary for the realisation of gender justice ... an increased level of economic independence for many women and an end to the gendered discriminatory nature of current welfare systems.'

Feminist economics, which grew in influence from the mid-1980s, encompassed a strong critique of the assumptions underlying the welfare state developments in Western Europe. It was argued that the link between paid employment and welfare entitlements – a fundamental element of most welfare states – reflected a perspective that showed a complete lack of recognition of the fluidity of women's economic activities. In practice, women's economic lives are likely to be shaped by a spectrum of economic activity: paid employment, home-based carer, part-time employment, underemployment and unpaid work. Such a fluid economic picture fell largely outside the male-oriented binary image of employment and unemployment that shaped Western welfare states.

The lack of recognition of unpaid work that has characterised mainstream economic thinking was the focus of Marilyn Waring's ground-breaking text *Counting for Nothing: What Men*

Value and What Women are Worth, which revealed the essential flaw of traditional gendered economic thinking.[25] At the heart of such thinking is the undervaluing of care and care labour – largely carried out by women – and the structural economic disadvantages experienced by women as a consequence. Essentially the male-worker/earner breadwinner model which rendered the majority of women as dependents within Western welfare states (and in relation to family income) was the dominant patriarchal welfare model – a model that penalised women for carrying the majority of care responsibilities. Linked to such gendered economic perspectives is a fundamental inequality in the sharing of unpaid work that has persisted up to the present day at a global level. The only exceptions to this have been in the Nordic countries where a significant majority of women entered the paid employment economy and built up welfare entitlements closely on a par with men.

A consequence of this evolution of welfare states and the rigid nature of the formal economy has been the development of a whole series of regulations in Irish and other welfare states that impose a complex and impenetrable gendered web of welfare entitlements: different levels of payments to different claimants; restrictive access to labour market and training; a hierarchy of child support payment rates; severe gender inequality in pension entitlements; differential withdrawal of related benefits, for example rent supports and medical cards. Predominantly women welfare claimants are, as a result, involved in a complex set of negotiations and visits to multiple offices, waiting in endless humiliating queues to access benefits, while at the same time managing care demands of mainly low income households.

Feminist debates on the benefits of basic income

One of the hugely beneficial effects of a basic income system would be that the unwieldy, ad-hoc evolution of gendered welfare states with their systems of inclusion and exclusion, of entitlement and non-entitlement could be dismantled and replaced by a basic income entitlement to all adults and without any of the restrictions of access to paid employment that are subject to policing under current systems. As Kaori Katada has argued, basic income is recognised as a 'payment for household and care labour ... however, perspectives on the impact basic income has on the gender division of roles and on the labour market differ'.[26] On the one hand is an argument that a rigid gender division of labour may be reinforced under a system of basic income or alternatively a counter argument is that those rigid gender roles may be challenged by the workings of a basic income model in practice. As basic income ensures that income is *unconditionally* paid to all citizens as an *individual right*, it may be argued that it would alleviate unequal distribution of income within the household and secondly, because there are no eligibility criteria other than age, a rights-based approach treating women and men equally would be put in place.

Unconditionality in this case means that eligibility would not be based on employment status, employment record, willingness to work or marital status and there would be no requirement to take a means test, work test or behaviour test in order to establish eligibility. This is likely to favour women who have found themselves excluded from active labour market programmes, pensions and a range of benefits because of an interrupted paid work history. In this context, one perspective within feminism asserts that basic income is a way of re-evaluating the economic value of the (paid and unpaid) work women have primarily been responsible for in the past, while also *promoting the economic independence of women*. A second perspective holds that a basic income model would return women to the home, and contribute to a backlash that runs *counter to women's liberation and independence*.

So, a key question from a feminist perspective is whether basic income promotes women's economic independence. Feminists have traditionally asserted that individualised welfare and other entitlements are indispensable to the exercise of women's socio-political rights and it may be argued that a basic income model supports that. By establishing women's autonomous guaranteed income, a basic income model breaks the tying of entitlements to paid wage labour. There is no guarantee, however, that additional household earnings above basic income, generated by paid employment or other income-generating activities, would be more equally distributed within a household or within wider society. So, from another perspective, the question is whether there is a danger that basic income may mean a permanent low income for many women in which gender inequalities may be reinforced or even exacerbated.

Some feminists have viewed basic income from a definite negative perspective. It is argued by some that firstly, by recognising the value of household and care labour and secondly, providing economic compensation for it, a basic income might suppress the demand for revaluing care work and trap women into the private space of the home, thereby maintaining and strengthening rigid unequal gender division of roles and labour. Feminists opposing basic income most often base their arguments on this kind of scenario.[27] From this different perspective, recognising household and care labour as an activity with socially beneficial value - as opposed to the payment for it - is essential for a feminist process of social change. It is argued that under this approach, it then becomes feasible that free and universal household and care services can become core public services providing high quality care and consequently the development of more equal gender roles.

Basic income together with equality policy measures

Dominant thinking within feminism is that basic income needs to be introduced *alongside other policies* that address and effectively challenge gender inequality in the division of labour, and more widely in the political-cultural systems. Feminists have highlighted the following concrete policies that need to be introduced together with basic income which encompass the following kind of changes:

· work sharing or reduction of labour time for all people
· gender equality of outcome in the labour market

- substantial maternity and paternity leave
- periodic or continuous leave for full-time care labour
- affordable high quality care services
- equal gender representation in decision-making
- changes in the culture and norms of the labour market
- effective policies addressing gender-based violence
- cultural shift away from sexual objectification of women.[28]

John Baker states that the important issue concerning the gender division of labour is the dominant ideology relating to gender, in which care labour continues to be considered to be the women's 'natural' role. In order to effectively challenge that ideology, in his view, a *cultural change* that makes care labour equal between men and women is needed. Baker's viewpoint is that men are currently penalised by their lack of access to care activity and women are also penalised by the expectation that they will carry the majority of care responsibilities.[29] Almaz Zelleke adopts a similar approach arguing that the focus of the discussion on whether or not basic income itself will promote the dissolution of the gender division of labour is an inadequate starting point. Instead, she argues that basic income should be seen as one critical element in promoting gender equality.[30]

Citizenship, democracy, basic income and feminism

Carole Pateman's work brings feminism together with political theory in relation to citizenship and democracy and, she argues also, a *guaranteed basic income* is a citizens' right. In her view, a basic income is part of a process of social change based on a just society eliminating social institutions and practices that produce *relationships of domination and oppression*. Basic income, she argues, as an unconditional social transfer that assures all citizens a subsistence income is a way to counter the subordination that stems from the capitalist organisation of production and the differential *access to political power generated by economic inequality*.[31] In Pateman's view, basic income is a core entitlement of citizenship, fundamental to the democratic commitment to making some form of political participation available to all.

Pateman further argues that the division of the two perspectives of feminism on the relationship between basic income and the gender division of labour are 'matters of level'. In her view, if the level at which basic income is set is too low, it is likely to result in the maintenance of status quo or even the strengthening of the gender division of labour. On the other hand, a relatively high level of basic income, she argues, could have a transformational function. Pateman herself offers as a definition 'a level sufficient for a modest but decent standard of life' as the appropriate level to establish basic income.

Basic income in itself may not be able to challenge the gender division of labour. However, it can bring about one critical condition necessary for the realisation of that gender justice objective: an increased level of economic independence for many women and an end to the gendered discriminatory nature of current welfare systems – of which Ireland is a prime example. In combination with key cultural changes that challenge traditional rigid gender roles, effective policies and practices to achieve a more equal distribution of paid and unpaid work, including a valuing of care work, are needed. Alongside a move towards a basic income model, legislation, policies and practices as well as a shift in dominant ideologies are more likely to achieve greater gender equality in economic activity at every level.

7

Women, motherhood and care

Vanessa Olorenshaw, UK

'The only answer is for the state, finally, to catch up
to its responsibilities to those who currently work for
free, risking personal and financial vulnerability to do
important work for the benefit of society.'

For all the economic arguments for basic income and for all
discussions about the right to leisure, art, music and basic
subsistence, the feminist element of the case for basic income
is one which speaks loud and clear for women. Why? Because it
helps to address the dilemma of unwaged work done by women
in the home, the family and the community.

We have had decades of feminism, yet we are now entrenched
in a neoliberal capitalist economic system and continue to
repeat a history in which 'women's work' has been devalued,
not counted and freeloaded upon by society. Western culture
is increasingly individualistic and the goals of 'independence'
and 'self-sufficiency' are practically unquestioned as benign. Yet
the reality of human existence is that we are *all* dependent on
others to some degree at different points in our lives and there
is an accompanying need for the existence of those willing and
able to meet the needs of the dependent. The young, the sick,
the disabled, the elderly and the dying: no less human, no less
worthy, yet reliant on care by others. However, those who care for

them are often unwaged or low paid. We could call their labour 'care work' or 'dependency work'.

A universal basic income goes some way to answer the question: what do we do about inevitable dependency work without rendering the carer (usually women) financially dependent on men or stigmatised as 'welfare scroungers' and thereby vulnerable and marginalised? It could address the dilemma of: 'How can we ensure that women who work as carers outside the paid economy have full citizenship, economic autonomy and the right to self-determination?' It could reflect the wishes of many women: 'How can we enable women who would like to care for their children but are financially prevented from doing so to retain an income in order to do so?'

The problem is that having children is seen as a 'lifestyle choice', the implication being that having children is the equivalent of buying a puppy. Yet, women produce something absolutely crucial for the survival of our species: the human race. When it comes to the care of children, it is crucial to the future wellbeing of our societies: 'other people's children' will become our daughters-in-law, our doctors, our law-makers and our grandchildren's teachers, and more. The work we do when we raise our children prepares them for a future as productive citizens. The work we do in the home has to be done by somebody – yet all the while it is predominantly women doing this work, as many wish to do, we are exploited for the concern for our children and the wish to be the one to care for them. Those of us who would desperately love to be able to care for our children instead of delegating the care to childcare providers are unable to do so because the financial penalties – the sacrifice of an income and the family tax penalty, for example – leave no other choice.

When it comes to women, one of the problems we face is the way in which work done within the home (domestic work, childrearing) and the community (helping at school, voluntary work) are seen as 'private sphere' and 'not work'. Feminism has some work to do in challenging these deeply entrenched attitudes.

The only answer is for the state, finally, to catch up to its responsibilities to those who currently work for free, risking personal and financial vulnerability to do important work for the benefit of society. Whether it does so by granting a living wage for carers, as advocated by The Wages for Housework Campaign for decades, or whether it accepts the basic income perspective as a first step, the state must at last recognise the need for carers to receive an income for the valuable work they do.

8

My own private basic income

Karl Widerquist, USA

'The most common objection to basic income is that it's supposedly wrong to give things to people who don't work for it, when actually, the economy already gives billions of dollars of unearned income to people who are already wealthy.'

I have a private basic income – a small, regular cash income without means test or work requirement. It's probably large enough to meet my basic needs. And I got it thanks to privilege, nepotism, and two big lucky breaks.

My first big lucky break happened in 2009 when Georgetown University hired me as a philosophy professor on their campus in Qatar. Georgetown-Qatar, funded entirely by the Qatar government, has to pay an enormous premium to get faculty to agree to live and work in Qatar. I get paid three times as much as my wife. I teach half as many classes. She's a full professor. I'm only an associate.

Qatar can pay more than US universities because of its own series of lucky breaks that put it in control of enormously valuable resources. Its position today comes largely from decisions made about a century ago, as the Ottoman Empire was breaking up. Britain and France arbitrarily drew lines on the map to create what became the states of the Middle East. Those lines eventually gave some of those states enormous amounts of oil and gas and left others desperately poor.

The joy of options

I 'earn' my salary by doing a job few others are both willing and able to do. To some extent wages compensate for other disadvantages of the job. But this equalisation is only partial and, more importantly, it only occurs among people with similar options.

I had better options than most people in the world. My white, American upper-middle class privilege gave me the opportunity to get the qualifications and the flexibility to take this job. For every highly paid professional 'expat' in Qatar like me there are maybe eight or ten extra-low paid 'migrant labourers', some of whom make as little as $200 a month. They live in dorms for years at a time, separated from their families. They are unfree to quit or to change employers. They are unfree to leave the country without their employers' permission.

I see these workers often. They clean the toilets at my university. They bring me tea if I want it. They are, on average, several inches shorter than me thanks to childhood malnutrition, because human resource companies in Qatar have scoured the earth looking for the most vulnerable, cheapest labour. There is no combination of hard work and grit that could have put any one of these workers in my position from their starting point in life – nor is there a combination of bad choices that could conceivably put me in their position from my starting point.

I receive a high salary because I was lucky enough to be in the position to serve the whims of rentiers – that is, people who own resources and the stuff we make out of them. There are exceptions but, on the whole, the highest paid people are those advantageously placed to serve the whims of wealthy people. Doctors who perform cosmetic surgery for rentiers make far more than doctors who treat malnourished children.

And the power of ownership

The real money isn't in doing stuff for the people who own stuff. It's in being one of the people who owns stuff. My chance to do that was my second big lucky break.

A few years before I left for Qatar, my brother returned to the Midwestern United States with a significant amount of money he'd saved while teaching English. With that money, he'd bought a couple of houses, fixed them up, and rented them out. Although he made a very good rate of return, he had no more money to invest. He had less money because he was now teaching underprivileged children in a public school in South Bend, Indiana, instead of teaching relatively wealthy people in Tokyo.

We were a perfect match. I had the money but not the time or skills. He had the time and skills but not the money. And as brothers we had a bond of trust. No one is going to give tens of thousands of dollars every year to some guy who owned a couple of houses and said he knew how to manage more, but I'd give it to my brother. Nepotism made my business possible.

I also benefited because the US tax structure is extremely favourable to business owners in general and landlords in particular. Capital gains are taxed far less than income, and people who don't need their income are taxed less than people who do. My brother needs to live off of the salary our business pays him, and so he pays income tax on it. My wife and I don't need the money we make from owning most of the business. We live off the salaries of our jobs, and reinvest virtually our entire share of the business. These reinvestments count as 'losses' and so officially we have never made any income or paid income taxes on our share of the business.

Making private basic incomes universal

My wife and I don't have enough property income to put us in the top 1%. But we could quit right now and be safely out of poverty with probably as much as the most generous basic income proposals on the table right now.

We have a basic income – a permanently growing basic income – not just for life, but forever. Because we own stuff we don't need, our society rewards us with more and more stuff every year. We don't have to do anything to get more every year.

We don't quit because employers have offered us jobs with good working conditions and pay that makes us significantly better off than living on our basic income alone. Most people in a similar position would do the same. If some people don't work when a basic income becomes available, we should consider the possibility that employers aren't paying high enough wages. My wife and I are not better humans than most of the world's poor. Our lucky breaks make us different from the poor. And those same lucky breaks make us similar to most other people with money.

Just because I benefit from the unfairness of our economic system doesn't make its rules any fairer. Those rules are not some natural feature of the universe. People made them. People can change them.

Why don't we?

Obviously people who own stuff have a great deal of political power, but there's more to it than that. Most people and policymakers do not understand the difference between rewarding people who do stuff and rewarding people who own stuff. Spending rewards production, but rewarding production is not the same as rewarding people who do things that make production happen. Everything humans produce is made from a combination of human effort and resources. Some spending rewards human efforts, but the biggest rewards go to the owners of resources and of the things we've made out of them in the past.

People like to think that owners are 'entrepreneurs' and 'job creators'. To some extent this is true. Entrepreneurs are owners who put forth effort to increase the value of what they own, and often what they do is valuable. But there are three reasons entrepreneurship can't justify the enormous inequalities in the world today.

1. **For owners, work is optional. For everyone else, it's mandatory.** Owners do not have to be entrepreneurs. They don't even have to be competent. They can hire competent people to manage their money for them. The amount of 'entrepreneurship' in my story was miniscule. It amounts to this. *I lucked into money. My brother knew what to do with it. I gave it to him.* For nothing more than that, I never need to work again. Neither will my successors.

2. **Most owners aren't really entrepreneurs.** Economists have a saying, 'the entrepreneur tends to become a rentier'. The reason is simple. The more money you make, the more it makes for you, and that part of your income will eventually outstrip the part from the things you actually do. As a human, you will eventually stop working, and so, you'll stop getting money for doing stuff, but your stuff will keep on making money forever.

3. **We can get entrepreneurship without the enormous rewards to ownership we have today.** Rewards were smaller a half century ago, but there was just as much entrepreneurship. What can I possibly have done in the seven years that I've been accumulating stuff to justify rewarding me and my successors with a perpetually growing stream of work-free income? In short, nothing.

Some people who read this story will probably accuse me of hypocrisy, saying something like, 'If you're an egalitarian, why are you rich?' If I wrote a similar description of the economy when I was poor, they'd accuse me of jealously. That's the catch-22 for people who complain about the rules of our economic system. You're either hypocritical and riddled by guilt or jealous and grasping for more.

I plan someday to use my money for the good of others instead of just for myself. But it's the system that needs to change. Individual owners giving away things at their whim will not fix the unfairness of the system. The rules must change.

We don't need to eliminate the market economy or property rights. We just need to realise that a lot of the income in the world today goes to the people who own resources and the stuff we've made out of them. Tax that unearned income and share it with everyone – a universal and unconditional basic income. The most common objection to basic income is that it's supposedly wrong to give things to people who don't work for it, when actually, the economy already gives billions of dollars of unearned income to people who are already wealthy. The problem is we don't share it.

A longer version of this article appeared in Beyond Trafficking and Slavery on 'openDemocracy', June, 2017: opendemocracy.net/beyondslavery/karl-widerquist/my-own-private-basic-income.

My own private basic income

9

Coming off the fence on universal basic income

Ruth Lister CBE, UK

'... for all my ambivalence, I am coming round to the idea of a UBI as a means of ensuring everyone a modicum of basic security in an increasingly insecure world.'

I've always sat on the fence when it comes to universal basic income (UBI). There's much that is attractive in an approach that, in its pure form, does away with means-testing and contribution tests to guarantee every *individual* a basic income in their own right. I've thus also always welcomed the debate about basic principles that proposals for a UBI encourage while not actually signing up to any of those proposals.

In part my reluctance to sign up in support has reflected an ambivalence around the total absence of any conditions attached to entitlement. On the one hand this absence represents the absolute guarantee of security that is so attractive and it challenges the contemporary fetishisation of paid work as *the* citizenship responsibility. It leaves it to individuals to decide how they divide up their time between paid work, caring, community and citizenship-focused activities, education, creativity, family and friends, leisure pursuits or just being, without being dictated to by an intrusive state. On the other hand, as Nick Srnicek and

Alex Williams warn in *Inventing the Future*, the work ethic is deeply ingrained into our identities.[32] Even for someone such as myself, critical of the fetishisation of paid work, it's not so easy simply to shrug it off. When Srnicek and Willams call for 'the right to be lazy', I find myself recoiling at the idea that other people should be required to subsidise that right. That doesn't mean I believe many would necessarily exercise it as, on the one hand, there are many reasons why people would nevertheless still want to undertake paid work and, on the other, even those who don't may be busy in other ways.

Nevertheless, such fears are why I have found the idea of a 'participation income' a potentially attractive compromise. Put forward by the Commission on Social Justice, published in 1994, and, more recently, the late Tony Atkinson,[33] it would allow for a more inclusive form of conditionality, based on making a social contribution, than do the rules currently governing entitlement to social security. As well as paid work or job search, participation would include education, training, caring or formalised voluntary work. However, I recognise that it might be difficult to operationalise without intrusive 'participation testing'.

My ambivalence about a total lack of conditionality underlies some of my (and others') practical political concerns too. In a political and economic culture that places such stress on 'something for something' how likely is it that UBI would gain the necessary political support? Without such support I've had two main worries. One is that if progressives focus all their energies on calling for a UBI, they suck energy out of more immediate, potentially more achievable reforms, which might in a more modest way help put the security back into social security. Alternatively, if UBI *were* implemented, I feared it would be at a level that provided an even less adequate income than now for those without other means.

My other major source of ambivalence lies in what UBI means from a feminist perspective. In their Compass report, Howard Reed and Stewart Lansley rightly argue that, by treating women as individuals rather than members of households, it potentially offers greater economic independence and would make it easier to escape abusive relationships. They suggest that 'importantly, a UBI would both acknowledge and provide financial support for the mass of unpaid work, disproportionately undertaken by women, in childcare, care for the elderly and voluntary help in the wider community'.[34] They are valid points. But the authors ignore the case *against* UBI put by some feminists.

It does not value care work as such because it provides financial support whether or not care work is being undertaken in the home. And without other measures, designed to shift radically the gendered division of labour between paid work and care and close the continued gender pay gap, it could undermine mothers' and carers' position in the labour market by encouraging them to stay at home full time (see Chapter 6). This is perhaps less of an issue than in the past now that women are more firmly established in the labour market. Nevertheless, in the UK in the context of universal credit, which creates a major disincentive for second earners, it is not to be discounted. So the case for a UBI should be combined with measures to encourage men to take on more of the role of caring through for instance enhanced parental leave earmarked for them and with a call for a shorter working week so that both women and men can more easily combine paid work and unpaid care work supplemented by a UBI. Such an approach also offers a riposte to those who argue that UBI is simply a palliative designed to sugar the pill for those thrown on to the scrap heap in a future world without sufficient paid work for all.

It's partly the prospect of such a world in the face of automation that has led many to argue that UBI is an idea whose time has come. I'm not sure that it's sensible to base the case for UBI primarily on this scenario; it can divert the argument into whether or not it's likely to materialise. Whereas it's possible to argue the case for UBI on the basis of *today's* labour market, which is increasingly failing to provide adequate security as detailed by Michael Orton.[35] It and the social security system, which was designed on the assumption that people are either in full-time work or out of work, are out of sync, universal credit notwithstanding. And this is one reason why I have grown more sympathetic to the calls for a UBI.

Another is that most proponents now acknowledge that any UBI introduced today would have to complement rather than replace existing benefits (see Chapter 30). While this makes it less attractive from the perspective of simplicity and significantly reducing means-testing, it allays my fears that people without other means would be left worse off than now. And, provided it is not allowed to act as an 'unhelpful distraction' as the Work and Pensions Select Committee recently warned,[36] it leaves space for complementary campaigns for more modest measures to put the security back into today's social security system. Indeed perhaps such campaigns could mobilise some of the energy that the campaign for UBI has attracted.

Thus for all my ambivalence, I am coming round to the idea of a UBI as a means of ensuring everyone a modicum of basic security in an increasingly insecure world. T.H. Marshall defined social citizenship as 'the whole range from the right to a modicum of economic welfare and security to the right to share to the full in the social heritage and to live the life of a civilised being, according to the standard prevailing in society'.[37] A potentially feasible modest UBI would not be sufficient to ensure the more expansive end of Marshall's range but it would at least provide that 'modicum of economic welfare and security'.

This was originally published as a Compass blog on 20 January 2017: compassonline.org.uk/universal-basic-income-coming-off-the-fence

Coming off the fence on universal basic income

PART II: TOWARDS TOMORROW'S SOCIETY

10

A new politics

Anthony Painter, Royal Society of Arts, UK

'We are trying to build tomorrow's society with the politics of today.'

Basic income is not a policy. It is not 'welfare'. Nor is it a magical solution to all manner of societal and economic changes. Basic income is something more difficult, challenging and profound than all these things. It is a new way of thinking about our relationships with the state and with each other. And that makes basic income a highly challenging proposition.

We are challenged to think about how society is changing and how we want it to change. Our politics has become fraught, divided and angry. How in such a context can a big intervention such as basic income become possible? Whatever the future economy that awaits us, and however technology will impact on jobs, income and wealth, what difference will basic income make? These are enormous questions that the quick rush to judgment our democratic debate fosters simply won't answer.

For me, basic income is a platform for people to live more creative lives. It provides a bedrock of security, enabling people to earn a more stable income, adapt and learn, support their families and their communities, and try something new like setting up a new business. Fundamentally, the idea is to support *better* work of all types, some unremunerated, and enable better lives and stronger human relationships as a result.

The design of any basic income system is crucial. It needs to encourage work *and* enable people greater power in the jobs market – including the ability to walk away from demoralising jobs. This would, for example, create new possibilities for trade unions and professional associations to push for better work. Basic income has to ensure individual freedom *and* encourage us to do more together. Basic income demands experimentation but its core principles are clear – a regular payment that is universal and unconditional.

We are trying to build tomorrow's society with the politics of today. A bridge to the future is needed. So basic income needs a movement – a pluralistic movement that reaches across political, ideological and interest divides. The best thing that those who consider basic income to be essential can do is widen the tent. That means being open, welcoming, accepting of well-considered criticism and reaching out.

Without this movement, basic income can't happen. It's too big and too challenging for the current national debate but that can change. Basic income advocacy will come in many forms. Big social change takes time but we can move in the right direction step-by-step. The first step is to widen the conversation.

The Royal Society of Arts has called for a citizens convention to start the work of building a common story around basic income. So how about it? Can we create such a convention – as Scottish devolutionists did from the 1970s onwards – and ensure that a wide cross-section of society is invited and comes along? Can basic income reach across our anaemic public debate and open a different idea about our collective future? If it can't, if we can't, then this wave may break before reaching the shore. Instead, let's build a politics that can craft a different future. Let's reach the shore.

A new politics

11

Universal basic income for the post-industrial age

Roope Mokka and Katariina Rantanen, Demos Helsinki, Finland

'... we suggest viewing basic income not as income, but as the capacity to produce and thus to participate actively in society. Capable of much more than just a simple "employment fix", basic income could help to create no less than a shared political vision for a future society.'

A universal basic income (UBI) is one of the hottest policy debates of the time. However, there is a great misunderstanding in why we should experiment with the policy. Many think of UBI as a way of enabling 'capacity to consume'. Yet, in the post-industrial age UBI should be seen as enabling 'capacity to produce and to be active in society'. Failing to see this difference will inevitably connect UBI to ailing structures and diminish it into a curiosity.

The various experiments in basic income that have been launched around the world offer the idea as a solution to automation, lack of disposable income, benefit traps or a bloated bureaucracy. In other words, the goal is to 'fix' various parts of the existing relationships between the state, the individual and capital. Currently, the technology-driven vision for our society can be summarised thus: let robots do the dirty work, let a small group of creative entrepreneurs come up with new solutions to emerging problems and the rest of us can live on a universal basic income and the odd jobs the platforms provide.

In the present political climate, however, such a vision could be seen as short-sighted. What people want are jobs for everyone, not basic income. In many countries the public expects this to happen through a return to a resurgent manufacturing industry: a modern-day version of the great industrial society of the past. The UBI movement needs to take this sentiment seriously. Work has been the major source of dignity: the sense of being needed as an active participant and co-creator of the society and its central institutions.

In what follows, we suggest viewing basic income not as income, but as the capacity to produce and thus to participate actively in society. Capable of much more than just a simple 'employment fix', basic income could help to create no less than a shared political vision for a future society. This perspective shifts our attention from automation and the increasingly rapid disappearance of (white-collar) jobs to the wider implications of what work has meant to us as a society.

Framed in the right way, basic income can become much more than a quick solution for changing employment markets, or the societal flavour of the month of techno-fantasists. As a new universal policy, it can ignite a new social movement and help to create a unifying vision for a post-industrial society: a vision of better and more active life, that recognises each person's contribution as valuable.

Basic income and four reasons to fear the future

Recent popular debate on the subject of basic income has coalesced around four lines of argument. First, a wave of statesmen and business leaders have voiced their concerns over a future society where robots have replaced at least part of the workforce. Secondly, a couple of decades from now, advances in artificial intelligence, for example, might lead to us creating more wealth than we could ever have imagined before. This wealth would accumulate in the hands of the entrepreneurs and investors, however, and as incomes drop the economy as a whole risks collapse.

A third concern relates to employment and incentives, an issue, for example, which dominates the thinking of the Finnish basic income experiment.[1] There, the central argument is that basic income will end the incentive structure of the current social benefits system, one, it is argued, that discourages people from working. In Finland – as in many modern welfare societies – an individual has to navigate a web of income-tested 'basic' benefits that are paid on top of one another. The joint effect of the layered benefits is that if a person who is receiving these benefits finds a job, work does not necessarily pay. Moreover, becoming an entrepreneur (or even 'working' actively in the voluntary sector) can lead to losing one's benefits entirely.

A fourth concern relates to the reduction of bureaucracy and administration. The transaction costs of means testing the receivers of benefits are significant. The idea of an unconditional payment can therefore be seen as one way of providing a more efficient welfare system. This is the reason why basic income is of interest to the 'liberal' end of the political spectrum, where streamlining the state is a major concern.

These four arguments for basic income are all relevant. That said, they are all based on a somewhat outdated concept of the relationship between the state, the individual and capital. In the post-war societal consensus, rapid growth united employers, workers and the state in a shared mission. The different formulations provided the basis for all the industrial societies of the West. In this 'social contract', economic growth bound together the interests of the state, the people and private capital: the state ensured a steady supply of labour for the employment markets; employers, for their part, supplied the state with taxable income, but also people with a sense of worth and income.

Central to this vision was the idea that work is something permanent and not working permanently is a temporary situation that requires interventions: benefit systems, insurances,

Universal basic income for the post-industrial age

healthcare, re-education and more. But now, the changes in work are not just changing work itself, but breaking this 'machine'. If you take work out of an industrial society, the interests of capital, the people and the state are no longer aligned. And that is a major problem.

Indeed, work is not just simply about income to individual citizens. It is more, from both a societal point of view and an individual point of view. Work relates to our sense of worth, identity and social cohesion, and it plays a part in the contract that has bound together employers, the workforce and the state. Steady jobs and professions have been so central to our societies that currently our main way of contributing to society happens via work.

However, current lines of argumentation see basic income as something that 'fixes' the income part of what is now happening to work. We propose looking at the big picture, outside the contracts, workplaces and employment markets. We are in a situation where technological progress and globalisation seem to have broken the connection between growth, productivity and human wellbeing.

To understand the present, we must understand the past

Currently, basic income is regarded mainly as a redistributive social policy instrument. As such, its foundation is often traced back to social rights, such as the right to social security and adequate social and medical services. The idea of a universal basic income, however, can be traced back further in history to the establishment of civil rights, a far older embodiment of universalism and a more foundational set of rights. The basic income discussion commenced probably for the first time in its current form around the time of the American and French Revolutions in the late 18th century.

The 'founding father' of the US and political theorist Thomas Paine proposed an early version of the basic income. Paine's argument centred on access to land. He argued that since land existed before man and was not created by man, it should belong to everyone equally: every individual has an equal right to land by virtue of being human. Paine proposed that this entitlement to an equal share of land should come in a monetary form: each man and woman should receive a lump sum of £15 when he or she turns 21. The amount was roughly two thirds of an agricultural labourer's yearly income in Britain at the time.

Paine's reasoning was echoed by the American Nobel laureate Herbert Simon at the turn of the 21st century. While Paine focused on land, Simon justified redistribution through the claim that a producer's output depends largely on human and social capital, such as shared values, scientific knowledge, trust and other social institutions. Following Paine, he argued that social capital belongs jointly to all members of society rather than specific individuals. Therefore, the producer should only be entitled to a relatively small share of the profit. The rest should be taxed and redistributed as a kind of basic income to all members of society. Simon even went as far as claiming that at least 90% of all wealth in rich countries derives from social capital.[2]

Indeed, much of the value in today's society is created, renewed and sustained by us as a collective: the shared culture with its practices and manners, the trust in others, the shared language, the meetings in public spaces, the ideas we overhear, the conversations we enter into, the ideas that are in the public domain and not protected by licences or patents. All of these factors are in addition to - as Paine observed - the limited natural resources that lie in the hands of the few. There is no way an economic system of any kind could identify and capture all the value (through, for instance, taxes or markets) generated by these common elements, and allocate it fairly in the complex system of value creation that the modern economy is. In this way, the fact that we collectively produce things that enable market production but lie outside the monetary system is another reason to treat basic income as a universal civil right, rather than as a quick fix for an ailing industrial society.

But what is the essence of this right? What does basic income in fact represent in Paine's argument? We argue land should be seen as representing a *capacity to produce*. In the rural society of Paine's era, land represented access to a means of production, or the ability to independently produce a harvest.

Capacity to produce in the 21st century

What is equal to land in the 21st century? What does the capacity to produce entail in a post-industrial society? To answer that question, we should look at basic income as capital, and not just money. Capital can be seen as all the physical and intangible assets that combine with labour to produce the goods and services in an economy (data, machines, offices, intellectual property rights, brands, energy and software). In other words, money becomes capital when we have enough of it to invest in what Karl Marx called 'means of production'.

Post-industrial means of production are very different to those in Marx's time of industrial revolution. The technology, economics and business scholars Erik Brynjolfsson, Andrew McAfee and Michael Spence point out that software-based products and services are changing the nature and the role of capital in relationship to labour.[3] Furthermore, they argue that technological progress speeds up the accumulation of wealth, with machines substituting for more types of human labour than ever before, creating more capital in the process. The real winners, the writers argue, are entrepreneurs who can create new solutions to new problems, while the rest will remain outside the new economy regardless of how much labour or traditional capital they can supply.

Here we have a great paradox on our hands: as a new kind of (digital) capital is becoming abundant and is replacing human labour in the production of goods and services, it is also slipping out of reach of most people. We are facing an era of abundance, in which the means of production are available to fewer people than before.

Therefore, we should see basic income not just as income for paying rent and buying food, but increasingly as access to capital in the productive sense of the word: in the same way as the right to own and claim land existed when moving from a feudal society to the era of nation states; and just as there was the right to healthcare and education after the move from an agrarian to an industrial society.

Now that we are moving from an industrial society to the next phase of socio-technological development, we have to ask what are the new rights people should have to remain active participants of society, to be able to produce, contribute and create value – not just to survive and have enough money for basic necessities, or, worse, to have state-sponsored jobs that could and should be automated.

In creating a new universal benefit system, we are building a new relationship between everyone. Therefore, the real question about basic income is a big one: why? What is the purpose of this relationship? Why should anyone get this money? This question of framing should not to be confused with introducing conditionality to basic income (thus destroying its core idea). It is merely a question of how to communicate the purpose of basic income.

In this, we should look to the founding fathers and their idea of basic income as an extension of ownership rights. And ownership not just to have, but ownership as a freedom to produce. Picture this: this time we are not fleeing the feudal society, but an industrial one. Our industries can no longer provide us with the means of production. Work and politics no longer supply us with adequate means of participation. We need to figure out nothing more or less than a new way of collaborating to create value.

12

A down payment on a new, cooperative economy

Avi Lewis and Katie McKenna, The Leap Manifesto, Canada

'In a way, basic income could also be seen as a down payment on a new, cooperative economy, a subsidy for more socially just economic activity, care-oriented work and political organising – much of which receives no compensation in the current economy.'

In 2015, over 60 movement leaders from Canada's Indigenous rights, social and food justice, environmental, faith-based and labour movements came together to write *The Leap Manifesto*[4], a roadmap for how Canada can transition away from fossil fuels in a way that changes the country for the better. The manifesto contains 15 demands to shape the great transition, and the thirteenth relates to a basic income guarantee:

'Since so much of the labour of caretaking – whether of people or the planet – is currently unpaid, we call for a vigorous debate about the introduction of a universal basic annual income. Pioneered in Manitoba in the 1970s, this sturdy safety net could help ensure that no one is forced to take work that threatens their children's tomorrow, just to feed those children today.'

So why this most Canadian of entreaties – a call for a *debate* – in this otherwise-declarative manifesto?

On one hand, for some environmentalists, feminists and advocates of Indigenous rights in this country, the progressive case for a basic income could not be more clear. An income is society's way of recognising an individual's contributions to the collective good. A basic income guarantee is therefore an acknowledgement of the value of the unpaid labour that underlies our collective wellbeing: the defence of our water, land and air; care of family and community – or as it's referred to in *The Leap Manifesto*, the labour of caretaking 'of people and the planet.'

A basic income set at a high enough level would also address the indignity and cruelty of our country's current poverty-alleviation programmes, where in the country's largest province, Ontario, recipients of social assistance survive on incomes that are *up to 60% below the poverty line*. As one recipient put it in an interview with the *Toronto Star*: 'Someone else decides when and if I eat.'[5]

Canada has also contributed a specific and fascinating chapter to the history of basic income. In the 1970s, the federal and provincial governments collaborated to run an experiment in Guaranteed Annual Income (GAI) in Dauphin, a rural municipality of 10,000 in Manitoba. From 1974 through 1978, all residents were eligible to participate, and approximately 30% of the city's population received, a 'mincome', or minimum income. If household income dropped below the amount equivalent to welfare rates at the time, the programme would top it up. Participants could use the money as they chose.

But the experiment ended prematurely in 1978, when a new provincial government was elected, and the findings were not analysed or written up. Two decades later, University of Manitoba researcher Evelyn Forget decided to find out what effect the programme had had on health and community life in Dauphin; she dug into the records to create a comparative study of the health care records of Dauphin's citizens from 1974 and

A down payment on a new, cooperative economy

1978 with those of the control group of people living in similar Manitoba communities at that time.

Forget found that compared with the control group, Dauphin residents living under the mincome experiment had a significant reduction in hospitalisation, admissions related to mental health, and accidents and injuries; physician contacts for mental health diagnoses fell overall, a greater proportion of high school students continued on to grade 12, and women took longer parental leaves.[6] 'In all of the indicators I could find for quality of life, people did better,' Forget told the *Toronto Star* in 2011.[7] The study concluded that even a modest GAI could lead to significant healthcare savings.

The unfinished Dauphin experiment looms large in the Canadian imagination around basic income, and bipartisan interest in the topic has continued since the 1970s. Several states are in the process of launching pilots (see Chapter 32).

In Canada, the recent momentum around basic income seems to be driven by a range of concerns: security for workers whose jobs are threatened by the growth of robotics and artificial intelligence, and frustration with the absurdly low levels of support, and bureaucratic means testing associated with current welfare programmes.

A recent survey across Canada by polling firm Angus Reid found that more than half of all respondents supported the idea of a basic income – but 60% felt it would be 'too expensive' to implement.[8] In short: Canadians support the idea of a basic income, but don't want to pay for it.

But not all progressives in Canada and elsewhere are on board with the growing enthusiasm for basic income. For some, the very fact of the support of various establishment forces for a basic income – from Friedrich Hayek and Milton Friedman in the past to Silicon Valley tech evangelists and neoliberal governments with a progressive veneer today – gives them pause. What is it that they find so enticing about this idea?

First, the purpose of guaranteed income for austerity-minded governments is to sweep away vast swathes of the social safety net, replacing all those overlapping social programmes (and all the attendant government jobs, with hard-won public sector salaries and pensions) with a streamlined bureaucracy. There is a real fear that – left to our current, captured political class – the implementation of basic income could become just one more rollback of the welfare state.

Second, as Ed Whitfield (see Chapter 21) of the US Fund for Democratic Communities points out, basic income has the immediate effect of increasing consumption, while changing nothing about underlying patterns of ownership, production, or distribution of wealth.[9] While it's true that the biggest problem for impoverished people is that they don't have money, in an ownership society, communities will not control their destinies until they control wealth, resources, and productive assets. A basic income does not advance this fundamental goal – in fact, it would require a monumental struggle that would sap social movement energy away from it.

Finally, given the racism and exploitation to which migrants around the world are treated, a basic income could easily be implemented as yet another benefit that is granted to those privileged with citizenship, while denied to those who grow their food, raise their children, and clean their tables.

Despite such reservations, there are other strategic reasons for leftists to advocate for basic income. While it may not immediately ensure democratic control of resources and productive assets, it might help shift the economy in a direction where that becomes possible in the future.

First, a basic income could strengthen the hand of the labour movement. Basic income will mean employers have greater difficulty filling jobs – and that increases the bargaining power of workers to better their conditions. Basic income would also serve as a kind of permanent strike fund – meaning that workers, considering striking on behalf of their rights or labour and environmental standards, would know they could fall back on basic income if they weren't receiving pay during a work stoppage.

Basic income could also help start to 'decommodify' our labour. People's labour is treated like an extractable commodity in the current economy – and so people are forced to sell it on the labour market to private firms or the state to gain a means of subsistence. We need to make the case that entitlement to an income and a dignified life should not be dependent on working for an employer, nor conditional on searching for employment. A basic income would free people from this compulsion, granting them much fuller freedom to direct their lives, engage in civic activity, or enjoy leisure time.

In a way, basic income could also be seen as a down payment on a new, cooperative economy, a subsidy for more socially just economic activity, care-oriented work and political organising – much of which receives no compensation in the current economy.

In October 2016, The Canadian Centre for Policy Alternatives (CCPA) published a 60-page compendium of varying perspectives on the potential for a basic income in Canada.[10] While positioning themselves as neither flagbearers nor opponents of basic income, the editors wrote that they chose to engage with the topic because of the unique public policy moment unfolding in Canada, a counterpoint to the 'deeply rooted cynicism about what we can achieve collectively ... [that] has long infused Canadian political thinking and policy making.'

Bolstering the power of collective action, expanding the sense of what's possible, and rejecting incrementalism for transformative change are the driving spirit of *The Leap Manifesto*, which closes with the lines: 'Now is the time for boldness. Now is the time to leap.' It's inspiring to see these values and that ambition reflected in how the respected progressive institution of the CCPA has framed the great national debate to come.

We live in a deeply unequal world, threatened by overlapping crises from climate change to structural racism to resource depletion. More and more people are coming to the conclusion that we have run out of time for anything other than change that reaches to the very roots of our system – the values that govern our world. Does basic income meet the measure of this historical moment? On the cusp of a major national debate in Canada, we and many of our fellow contributors to *The Leap Manifesto* are engaging with open hearts – and open eyes.

A down payment on a new, cooperative economy

13

Basic income: a solution to which challenge?

Brenton Caffin, Nesta, UK

'So, what if we started by reframing basic income as citizen equity? A collective investment by all of us, in you and every citizen.'

A universal basic income is an income unconditionally granted to all on an individual basis, without a means test or work requirement. It has been proposed at various times over the centuries by a great variety of thinkers. Two years ago, Nesta predicted that we would be hearing a lot more about basic income.[11] However, the rising interest has been beyond astonishing. Figure 13.1, with data from Google Trends, shows the great jump in interest in the last four months of 2016 alone.

Basic income conversation can be viewed as an unlikely alliance between different interest groups. In one corner, there are the venture capitalists dreaming of a future of mass automation, robotics and algorithms, and the inherent massive disruption of existing labour markets this will cause. In another, the radical left advocating a new universal compact - addressing the challenges of market driven inequality and the rise of the 1%. Finally, there are the imagineering bureaucrats - seeking to rationalise the state and the complexity of managing the

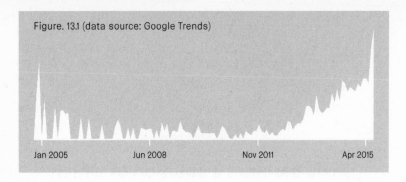

Figure. 13.1 (data source: Google Trends)

Jan 2005   Jun 2008   Nov 2011   Apr 2015

multiplicity of welfare provision through the provision of UBI and, in doing so, seeding market based welfare provision as opposed to state driven services and goods.

All of these motivations are valid and should be welcomed with the ideas developed alongside each other instead of against each other. We recognise that basic income has the capacity to address many of these challenges. However, we believe that, if implemented with the right intentionality, universal basic income has the potential to unlock even more value.

More than the redistribution of wealth in an increasingly structurally unequal world. More than a mark of solidarity to suggest 'we're all in this together' in an age of austerity. And more than a way to just simplify the welfare state.

It can and it should be more. We just need to dream a bit bigger.

What's in a name?

So, what if we started by reframing basic income as citizen equity? A collective investment by all of us, in you and every citizen.

What if we understood it as a new architecture of sovereignty and freedom? Economic sovereignty was a fundamental cornerstone of participation in democracy of the 19th century. We now have an opportunity to reframe this economic sovereignty and with it democratic participation fit for the 21st century. The impact of this sovereignty can significantly empower massive labour market liquidity; an unlocking of latent potential and innovation, which is currently locked up by a lack of opportunity.

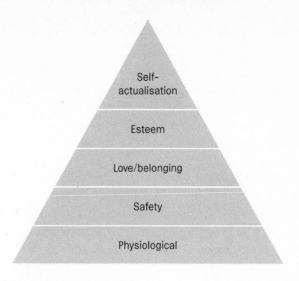

Figure 13.2: Maslow's hierarchy of needs

Democratising the purpose-rich economy where everyone can pursue their vision for a better world, thereby supporting the economy to better align capability and need with value creation.

What if we understood citizen equity as a massive extension of the Californian start-up economic model? A new model to unleash innovation capacity and with it a new typology of innovation. Beyond innovation for basic subsistence and survival (or ostentatious luxury to publicly prove independence from poverty); instead focusing our innovative capacities beyond the bottom half of Maslow's pyramid (see Figure 13.2) towards a fuller sense of self actualisation and all the benefits that come when citizens are achieving this. As Abraham Maslow put it, 'What a (wo)man can be, (s)he must be.' [12]

This is a model in which the source of social recognition and reputation is in creating real world innovations and change that improve people's wellbeing. It challenges the notion of capitalist consumption acting as the ultimate legal high and end goal of an economy. It gives us the opportunity towards a market which unlocks the capacity of all citizens to imagine a new class of human 'goods' and 'services' which seek to fulfil human needs and desires as yet unproduced. It could seed a new epoch of

Basic income: a solution to which challenge?

75

supply and demand which transcends the dichotomy of essential and luxury goods on which so much current innovation is based.

In this way, citizen equity could unleash a huge new democratic enlightenment revolution, a new inclusive economic paradigm. Here is a new potential to do what Henry Ford did at an unimaginable scale – but this time for social innovation not merely consumption.

A new social contract?

Seen through the intentionality of citizen equity, basic income can be a way to change the social contract of welfare. Going beyond the language of rights, it can reframe welfare as a collective investment which seeks to unlock a new economic and innovation revolution. It seeks to unleash a renewal of democratic sovereignty and enfranchisement worn down by consumption fatigue and competition-based economies.

Fundamentally, these radical hypotheses are about reconceptualising basic income not merely as a new safety net but instead a universal trampoline. A societal investment to unlock our individual and collective potential where we are all thereby obliged to provide societal return of civic investment. To create the breathing space for even more 'New Radicals'.[13]

To reimagine our 1950s welfare state we need a real moon shot worthy of our age – a real Star Trek idea to match our Tricoders. Currently basic income is just a dream but basic income as citizen equity is a dream worth dreaming.

14

What we talk about when we talk about work

Olivia Hanks, Norwich Radical, UK

'A guaranteed, subsistence-level income would end extreme poverty and allow people time to look for meaningful work instead of relying on jobs that are short-term, insecure and exploitative.'

'What do you do?' I could give a lot of answers to this question. I cook. I grow vegetables. I campaign for a political party. I write poetry and then put it away in a drawer. But the question really meant by these words is 'What do you *get paid* to do?'

Most of us define ourselves by our paid work. It's what we spend more time doing than anything else. And the rest of our time is often defined by work: travelling to it, recovering from it, or lapsing into total lethargy during holidays as a reaction to it. Yet a 2013 Gallup poll of 142 countries showed that only 13% of people feel engaged by their jobs.[14]

This source of unhappiness and waste of human potential has led some to argue that the ideal would be to abolish work.[15] This may be taking things a little far, even if we take 'work' to mean only 'paid employment' – I wouldn't like to abolish doctors, for instance. Nevertheless, it gets us thinking about what work really is.

Until the industrial revolution, most people were subsistence farmers, working to produce what they needed and no more. Work as a transaction – time in exchange for money – only became widespread with industrialisation and the mass movement of people into the cities in the 19th century. There, people had no access to land to provide their food, so were forced to 'earn their living' in factories, gaining only a fraction of the fruits of their labour as reward.

Though working conditions in the UK have improved dramatically, this state of affairs remains fundamentally the same for employees today. The idea that your 'living' is something you have to 'earn' persists, for the most part quite unchallenged. Yet many people would freely admit that they see their job as essentially pointless. Phrases like 'earning a living' and, more recently, 'hardworking families' or the rhetorical division of citizens into 'strivers' and 'skivers' reinforce the view that paid employment is a virtue, and the more hours of it you do, the better. Other useful or fulfilling types of work such as caring and community work are disregarded.

The anthropologist David Graeber writes in a 2013 essay that 'bullshit jobs' have been created because 'the feeling that work is a moral value in itself, and that anyone not willing to submit themselves to some kind of intense work discipline for most of their waking hours deserves nothing, is extraordinarily convenient' for the ruling class.[16] This is almost an exact echo of the opening of William Morris's 1884 lecture 'Useful Work Versus Useless Toil':

> 'Most people, well-to-do or not, believe that, even when a man is doing work which appears to be useless, he is earning his livelihood by it – he is "employed," ; and most of those who are well-to-do cheer on the happy worker with praises, if he is only "industrious" enough and deprives himself of all pleasure and holidays in the sacred cause of labour. In short, it has become an article of the creed of modern morality that all labour is good in itself – a convenient belief to those who live on the labour of others.'[17]

Graeber's repetition of these thoughts well over a century later, despite the advances in productivity during that time, shows that this is not a question that will ever be solved by more technology or ever-greater productivity – it is clearly a political matter.

Much has been written about the impact on jobs of the new wave of automation. Yet despite the widespread concern about the impact on employment, previous waves of automation have not led to a hike in unemployment. Instead, directly productive jobs now done by machines have been replaced by Graeber's 'bullshit jobs' in the clerical, sales and service sectors. Unless we change the way we think about work, we will simply end up with a new generation of meaningless jobs to replace those lost; another generation of workers stuck in jobs they do not like and of which they do not see the point. If we see unemployment as the problem, as artificial intelligence renders vast numbers of jobs obsolete, we risk seeing the creation of a new wave of 'bullshit jobs' as the solution.

Instead, we should seize upon the growth of artificial intelligence (AI) as the ideal opportunity to introduce a universal basic income, alongside a more progressive system of taxation. A guaranteed, subsistence-level income would end extreme poverty and allow people time to look for meaningful work instead of relying on jobs that are short-term, insecure and exploitative. Recognising that material wealth comes from the earth's resources and belongs to society as a whole, it would more fairly distribute the wealth created by technological advances, rather than concentrating that wealth in fewer and fewer hands.

When we no longer see paid work as an immediate necessity for survival, other reasons for working will come to the fore: intellectual challenge or physical fitness, social interaction, the sense of doing something useful. Once the financial imperative to accept poor pay and conditions has vanished, workers will start demanding that their jobs fulfil some of these other needs.

UBI would also give people more choice about how much they work. The result would be better health, both physical and mental; better family life, as parents are no longer forced by financial necessity and social pressure to go back to work at the earliest possible opportunity; and more engagement with politics and community life. Paid employment would no longer be the only or principal determiner of people's identity, status and self-esteem.

One of the most common arguments against UBI is that large numbers of people would give up work. This rests on two assumptions: first, that most people only work for the money, and would stop working if they could; second, that people leaving the workforce would be a terrible thing.

The first is unlikely to be the case: most people want to work in some form. Insofar as people do work 'only for the money' because they have meaningless, unfulfilling jobs, the greater bargaining power would make employers offer more appealing jobs, whether through improved pay or other means. And while UBI would be sufficient for survival, it would not pay for a life of material comfort. Those who wanted more would still need to be part of the paid workforce.

Given that there are always concerns about a shortage of jobs, it cannot logically be argued that some people withdrawing from the workforce would cause society to collapse. Rather, the second assumption is based principally on the belief that everyone has a moral duty to 'pay their way' financially, and that any other system is unfair. This is a symptom of the tendency of modern political discourse to place the economy above all else; to refer to it as though society existed to serve its needs, and not the other way round. UBI implicitly recognises a fundamental point: that paid work has no intrinsic value, and that not all valuable work is paid. Many people contribute in other ways, as carers, as artists or as volunteers; some people are simply unable to work full time, and UBI would enable those people to live dignified, meaningful lives.

What I am really arguing for here is more time. What I ideally want to see is a reduction in the working week;[18] but that is harder for government to implement and risks being seen as authoritarian. In the meantime, UBI would at least give people the choice to work less, or to take time out of work. When we can meet our basic needs without selling our labour, we take control of our own time. Paid employment, when we are freed from the crushing weight of compulsion, can become just one way among many in which we choose to give meaning to our lives.

15

It's time to stop tinkering

Jonathan Bartley and Caroline Lucas MP, Green Party, UK

'To seize this moment those of us who believe in social solidarity need a big idea.'

These are worrying times for those of us who believe in a welfare state that supports people from the cradle to the grave. In the past seven years, under the cover of a global financial crisis, the British government has accelerated the scaling back of the state, a process that began in the early 1980s, and has gradually chipped away at social security provision. Housing benefit has been slashed, child benefit is no longer universal and many of the services that people rely on in their communities – from libraries to children's centres – have been sacrificed at the altar of austerity. Where there used to be a state-provided safety net, there are now foodbanks in every major town and city in Britain.

The world of work is also in the grip of a crisis. Real wages are still lower than they were ten years ago – a staggeringly long slump. And, while unemployment didn't rise as expected after the financial crash, a shadow economy has grown which sees people 'in work' but without the security of a regular job. The 'gig economy', as it is known, can mean liberation for highly paid freelancers but, more frequently, it means factory workers not knowing when their next shift is, delivery drivers spending hours of unpaid time waiting for work that isn't guaranteed to materialise. Vast numbers of people are underemployed – searching for more hours to get by. In a globalised world – and especially in this post-referendum era – where workers in Britain are competing not only with each other but with others across the world, a race to the bottom might keep us 'competitive'. Increasingly flexible working might sound like a positive development but the fact is that it's fraught with risks for workers.

If the world of work seems tough now, experts are saying that it might get even tougher. You only have to walk into a supermarket, where you're as likely to be served by a machine as a fellow human being, to see how technology that was unimaginable just a few years ago has replaced jobs upon which people relied. Think of the impact of driverless cars and lorries – and the serious repercussions that such a change would have on our economy: no lorry drivers, no cab drivers – just smart computers ferrying goods and people where they need to go.

The picture we've painted above might not fill readers with hope, but it is our belief that a phoenix could rise from the ashes of the broken system we have now. When Keynes predicted that automation could set people free in the 20th century he was wrong, but only in his timing. The coming automative revolution could lead to waves of unemployment, poverty and an ever more divided society – or it could liberate people from the drudgery of work and give them more time for the things that matter. But to seize this moment those of us who believe in social solidarity need a big idea, to counter the potential race to the bottom on wages and rights that could come from automation.

In their book *Inventing the Future*, Nick Srnicek and Alex Williams take aim at what they call 'folk politics'.[19] The term refers to the many movements that have sprung up against modern-day capitalism, perhaps best exemplified by the 'one no, many yeses' which defined the anti-globalisation movement. While our party's traditions are very much defined by 'bottom-up' action – from protests to co-ops, we share the belief that

It's time to stop tinkering

progressives desperately need to coalesce around a big idea to counter the neoliberal hegemony that's infected our politics and economics for half a century. Like them, we believe that a basic income will be at least part of the answer to the big questions of today.

Not only will a basic income re-establish the safety net that the crumbling welfare state no longer provides and protect people from the perils of the modern job market, but – as the level of payment rises – it will also give people the security to be liberated rather than enslaved by technology and choose how much time to spend in traditional 'work'. We should not be defensive when we talk of a basic income. Yes, it will protect people but, crucially, it also has the potential to set them free.

Ultimately basic income challenges the idea that we are first and foremost producers and consumers, economic units that must drive endless growth. It's such an exciting idea because it will help us form a clearer idea of what constitutes welfare, good work and human flourishing, and it would help us towards a more balanced economy which acknowledges what is truly 'productive' in its broadest sense.

Of course plotting a path towards implementing a basic income is not without its challenges. One clear and present danger is the adoption of the policy by those who wish to use it as cover to further erode social security and our public services. Progressives who advocate for a basic income have to be crystal clear from the start: it will not replace our public services, nor will it mean an end to additional support for people who need it. Crucially basic income, and a shorter working week, must come alongside rising wages – to bring an end to underemployment by ensuring that people's working hours plus basic income provide them with what they need. Similarly, with the housing market in Britain so dangerously overheated and young people particularly struggling to pay for the roof over their head, a rent cap is needed too.

Basic income, which has often been dismissed as utopian, is making its way into the mainstream. The Alaskan version of the idea – an annual social dividend, in this case funded by oil revenues – has been in place since the 1980s.[20] Trials are under way in several countries (see Part V), and there is support from a range of organisations from the pressure group Compass to the 'innovation charity' Nesta. Who would have thought, just a few years ago, that a Labour Shadow Chancellor – John McDonnell – would be open to exploring the idea of a universal basic income?

A number of models for the basic income exist – and all need further investigation. But the bottom line is that it's crucial that any shift towards this bold new policy protects and increases the income for the poorest and those who aren't able to work.

Some say the basic income sounds too good to be true – and that it's unaffordable. The exact cost, of course, would depend on the level of payment but what is clear is that shifting to a universal payment would significantly cut the cost of administering the many different types of means-tested benefits we have at present. Crucially this is a policy designed to be redistributive – costing those with the most money more.

Britain in the 21st century is home to both a growing number of foodbanks and a growing number of entrepreneurial pioneers. Fewer and fewer of us are engaged in traditional 9–5 jobs at the office or factory – for reasons both good and bad – and that means increasing amounts of uncertainty. Social security is called that for a reason, yet it hasn't kept pace with the changes to our work economy – and it's become increasingly clear that we need to do more than simply tinker around the edges of the system.

For those who oppose basic income, but worry about our increasingly stratified society and precarious economy, we simply ask: if not this, then what? Through what other means can we both achieve genuine security and, over time, liberate people from the drudgery of work?

We are not naïve enough to think that a basic income will come about overnight – implementing it will take time and considerable research. That's why we're calling on the government to take the simple step of running a pilot of the scheme here in Britain, and investing in the serious research needed ahead of such a scheme to give it the best chance of success.

The basic income is a cornerstone of Green Party policy – and has been for decades – but we're not in the slightest bit concerned

It's time to stop tinkering

that the idea has been taken up by so many others. Indeed we look forward to working with progressives from across politics and civil society in making the case for this most ambitious of policies.

16

How I learnt to stop worrying and love basic income

Jonathan Reynolds MP, Labour, UK

'In this age of astonishing political volatility, politicians shouldn't be afraid to embrace radical ideas. That's why I came out for basic income – and why I think it must be part of the debate going forward.'

In early 2016, using the freedom from collective responsibility that I had recently attained by leaving the Labour frontbench, I wrote an article for the *New Statesman* entitled: 'How I learnt to stop worrying and love basic income'.[21]

For some time I had maintained a closet interest in UBI, and felt the time was now right to talk openly about why it appealed. But writing this piece was not without reputational risk. I was acutely conscious it would be written up as 'mainstream MP backs non-mainstream idea'.

Yet the reaction was extremely positive. I attribute this to two principal things: first, concerns about how the welfare state is operating at present in the UK; and second, concerns about how the welfare state might survive the transition into the future, especially in a world of automation and digital self-employment.

But as well as both of these I wanted to address the challenges faced by politicians on the left when it comes to rapid economic change and the impact that can have.

My outlook on politics is fundamentally shaped by my experience of growing up in the North East of England in the 1980s. The closure of entire industries, like coal and shipbuilding, had dramatic and fundamental consequences for the areas built around them. The same is true of the areas that have lost elements of the steel industry today. I still believe the Thatcher government's abject response to deindustrialisation lies at the heart of many of the problems the UK faces, such as low skills, worklessness and poor public health. The UK spent a fraction of what other countries, such as Sweden, spent on education and retraining as traditional industries declined, and we have suffered the consequences.

The left no longer has a convincing answer to how it should respond to seismic economic change. The traditional response, calling for the nationalisation of failing industries, doesn't solve the problem. Running an industry at a loss because it is subsidised by the taxpayer is not a long-term answer. Globalisation means it was inevitable that the UK would have to exit some traditional industries – I wouldn't fancy bringing back the industries of the first industrial revolution to Stalybridge, for instance – and education and retraining to take part in new economic opportunities are the only solutions. But as technology and the growth of the MINT countries – Mexico, Indonesia, Nigeria and Turkey – brings ever more economic disruption, as well as opportunity, we must have a mechanism to provide people with both security and a platform from which to be able to access these new opportunities. Basic income would do just that. This was the beginning of my interest in UBI – as a policy to cope with inevitable but fundamental economic change.

Then, when I was elected as a constituency MP, I began to come face to face with the problems of the existing welfare state every week in my advice surgeries. I have always been taken aback by the bewildering complexity of our welfare system. The Child Poverty Action Group's *Benefits Handbook,* which, like many MPs, I use to help constituents, is bigger than my copy of the Bible. And the modern incarnation of the welfare state – conditionality, sanctions, and adults being forced to fill in job search diaries as if they were in primary school – I find unconscionable. I don't deny there are a small group of people who do need a stimulus to enter the labour market. There are also people who definitely need to access some support to get back into work, especially with numeracy and literacy. But why should this be punitive? A system that sanctions war veterans for selling poppies, or a person for attending a job interview, is both ridiculous and counter-productive. And that's before we consider the fundamental problem of our current benefits system – how to taper off benefits when someone does return to work to ensure there is an incentive to work and not a 'benefits trap'.

The government's answer is universal credit. Having been in one of the pathfinder areas for universal credit, I'm afraid they will be disappointed. Thanks to former Conservative chancellor, George Osborne, universal credit will not now offer the kind of work incentives it was hoped it would, but the real problem is that it still cannot cope with the real nature of people's working lives. There is not, as much as some Tory MPs would claim, a big group of people who never work and then a larger group who pay their taxes to support these people. Instead, many people move frequently into and out of work, because the work they can get is short-term, or insecure, or because the other responsibilities in their lives cause complications. The benefits system simply cannot cope with these people, and nothing I have seen suggests universal credit will be a solution to that. But there are also huge questions regarding conditionality as the nature of work changes: if technology like Uber creates a hypothetically unlimited amount of self-employed work, how will conditionality work? Will every job seeker be forced to do self-employed work in exchange for their meagre support? It's a problem which is almost upon us now, and will only get more urgent.

My final reason for backing basic income is far simpler. I object to the levels of poverty in this country and believe them to be an indefensible waste of talent and resources. I wonder how many successful businesses, or technological inventions, or medical breakthroughs, we miss out upon because we do not give enough people the platform from which they might fulfil their potential. Just think how much more competitive the UK might be in the global economy if we stopped doing this. There is no Conservative understanding of the person who works two or three jobs but is still low paid, or who has had a successful career for many years but then fallen on hard times. Our current response to a scale of these problems is simply insufficient.

There are many issues still to resolve about basic income, such as how to give additional support to those with disabilities, and how to tackle the chronic British problem with housing benefit when we simply do not have sufficient houses. The vast differential in housing costs across the UK defeated even Beveridge, and the situation is much worse today. We would also need to consider how long economic migrants would have to be in the UK before they became eligible.

Now, as a member of Labour's Shadow Treasury team, I have had the opportunity to move this work forward with the creation of our working group on UBI, established in 2017. The group brings together advisers, academics, unions and policy experts in a forum for discussion about how a workable UBI proposal could be designed for today's welfare challenges.

I am convinced that many fundamental problems in the UK – be it dealing with economic change, work incentives, poverty or a lack of competitiveness – could be tackled in this way. I also think it provides an answer to one of the perennial questions for the Labour Party – how is it that the public loves the NHS yet resents the benefits system? The answer is, I believe, that the NHS provides something for everybody. So should the rest of the welfare state – providing again real social security for all. In this age of astonishing political volatility, politicians shouldn't be afraid to embrace radical ideas. That's why I came out for basic income – and why I think it must be part of the debate going forward.

17

Trust trumps control

Uffe Elbæk, Alternativet, Denmark

'If the freedom created by capitalism turns into a lack of freedom for the majority of the people, we must formulate new answers.'

Let us be blunt: unconditional basic income for all will not become a reality in Denmark anytime soon. But still, the prospect looks a lot brighter today than it did just a few years ago. Thanks in part to the efforts of Alternativet, basic income is once again on the political agenda in Denmark and is up for debate in much wider circles than we have seen in decades.

It is safe to say that more and more view UBI as one of the options worth exploring and experimenting with in the light of rapid automation and robotisation. That is a start.

But before I discuss the viability of unconditional basic income – or something like it – in Denmark, I should offer a few insights into the Danish context.

As most people know, Denmark is a modern welfare state relying on a massive and broad redistribution of wealth though a progressive taxation system. Based on the so-called Nordic model, the Danish welfare system aims to create economic security and opportunity for all within an elaborate social safety net.

Alternativet is a new progressive Danish political party formed in 2013 to champion a green agenda and sustainable development. The party is an expression of new political movements, such as the alter-globalisation movements, and local community projects and embracesa new horizontal and bottom-up politics rather than the dominant vertical and top-down politics of the past. It gained 4.8% of the vote in the 2015 general election and has 10 MPs in the Danish Parliament.

A key instrument in this is the flexible Danish labour market. Here it is easy and cheap for companies to fire employees – but generous unemployment payments mean people can sustain themselves until they find a new job. In other words, the 'flexicurity model' offers both flexibility for companies and security for the people.[22]

The system has only been successful due to a well-defined and very broadly accepted social contract of rights and duties. We all have the right to receive fair and adequate salaries and get financial support to be able to live good lives, even if we are disabled, sick or unemployed. On the other hand, it is our duty to educate ourselves and make ourselves available to contribute to the extent we can, which includes, to some extent, taking the jobs we are offered.

Because of this, because of our combined efforts and our shared dedication to solidarity, education in Denmark is not only free but you also get monthly grants to cover expenses. Health care is free, too. And if you lose your job you are not on your own: you will be supported financially for two years. After two years, the payments decrease, but they are still much higher than in most other countries.

This is the welfare state in action. Not because it wants to be generous, but because there has been a common understanding in Denmark that investment in people pays off. Today, government transfers benefits worth around 350 billion DKK a year, roughly €8,500 per Dane, per year.

This system has worked well for decades and is perceived as having secured prosperity and progress until now. But the social contract has been under increasing pressure in recent years as globalisation has left its mark on Denmark, the European Union and the world. The flexicurity model, too, is at risk of losing its dynamic as more and more struggle to find a place in an increasingly specialised labour market or imagine what their place could be in the future.

If these trends continue – and the evidence points to just that – we need to re-evaluate and re-organise the way our society functions. If the freedom created by capitalism turns into a lack of freedom for the majority of the people, we must formulate new answers, just as we did with the flexicurity model to create better lives in the industrial era.

In Alternativet, formulating these solutions for a still unknown, but perhaps radically different future is one of our main priorities. In an effort to share what looks like fewer jobs in the future, we have proposed a 30-hour working week – down 7 hours from the current 37-hour week. This could also combat the stress epidemic and secure a better work–life balance.

We are also exploring fourth sector ideas to create new ways of organising ourselves across society, including the possibility of time banking initiatives in which citizens are awarded time credits for voluntary activity from baby-sitting to gardening. It is within this bigger picture context that, at our 2017 annual meeting, we got the mandate to explore proposals for specific experiments with unconditional basic income that could be initiated on a small scale across Denmark.

One of the main challenges in designing such an experiment is that Denmark already has a high level of welfare for all. To have a real effect – for unconditional basic income to fulfil its promise of freer (if not wealthier) lives, for it to be a real answer to jobless growth and the challenges coming towards us – we will have to think long and hard on what will make sense in a Nordic style welfare state. And these answers – if we find them – will be radically different from the answers needed in the UK or the USA where government benefits are already far less generous than in Denmark.

In the light of this, one of the things we have proposed already is a reform of the unemployment system. Today, a whopping 74% of the resources spent in the Danish unemployment system is spent on bureaucratic control of the unemployed who have to apply for a number of jobs on a weekly basis (even where there is no match between the job and the applicant) and fill out numerous forms. Only 26% of the resources are directed towards contact with the unemployed and the corporations that could hire them.

In Alternativet, we believe this is a royal waste of money and resources. Control and mistrust of people does not motivate or help them to create better lives for themselves. But trust does: it encourages people to grow; gives them a chance to live up to their full potential. Our simple belief is that trust trumps control.

In the Danish municipality of Kalundborg, for example, they have dropped all types of control of the long-term unemployed. Instead, they are experimenting with unconditional benefits. At the same time, they are reinvesting the resources saved on not controlling the unemployed in better counselling and other efforts to improve their lives. To date the results have been very positive. The unemployed show much more initiative and twice the national average are activated – proving our belief that trust trumps control.

In Alternativet, with the lessons learnt from Kalundborg in mind, we have proposed a nationwide slashing of the time-consuming and costly control regime that is minimising the time the unemployed can spend on actually getting a job or educating themselves to be better fit to take a job.

The proposal has had a mixed reception from across the political spectrum, but we sense a general willingness to experiment more, as in Kalundborg. Most agree that the current control regime is, itself, out of control and needs to be re-evaluated and ultimately fixed.

As Alternativet prepares to develop ideas for specific experiments in Denmark, some prominent Danish business leaders are embracing the idea of unconditional basic income for all. These include the chief economist of SaxoBank, which is one of the more ideological – and pro-libertarian – banks in Denmark, strongly pro-market and small state. Of course, although some business leaders support the idea of a UBI as a way of dumping parts of the wider welfare state, their intervention also helps to fuel the discussion.

Despite our short history – we were founded in 2013 – Alternativet has been able to promote debate and help shift public opinion in ways we didn't imagine was possible. And we plan to continue to do so when it comes to the possibilities of unconditional and universal basic income.

We do so to continue our fight for an economy that creates surpluses on not just one but three bottom lines: the economic bottom line – still the dominant political discussion today; the social; and the environmental bottom line. The multiple crises we face demand exactly that. The future we are facing demands exactly that.

For unconditional basic income to work, at least from our point of view in Alternativet, it should – in interaction with other initiatives – serve as the opportunity to realise the dream of freedom and equality in a sustainable society.

Trust trumps control

PART III: DISSENTING VOICES

18

Why basic income can never be a progressive solution

Francine Mestrum, Belgium

'Many bridges can be built between the basic income idea and social protection. The priority should be minimum incomes for the poor, decent pensions and family allowances, universal health care and quality education.'

In an article (reproduced as Chapter 23) on basic income, Philippe Van Parijs mentions three major objectives: enhancing individual freedom, promoting universal rights and procuring economic security.[1] I fully share these objectives but claim that basic income is not the way progressives will want to realise them.

Individual freedom is extremely important but can never be dissociated from collective responsibility. In fact, this focus on individual freedom shows that basic income is fundamentally a liberal proposal. Progressives will always point to the collective, social dimension of all our needs and to the interdependence of all people. This is a different philosophy with direct consequences for the division of labour. There certainly is a need for more leisure time and for a drastic reduction of working hours, but there is also socially necessary labour that should be shared by all. By focusing only on individual freedom, many advocates of basic income forget that individual rights cannot exist or lose their meaning without collective rights.

Basic income should be a *universal right*. Our rights are indeed universal, as is said in the Universal Declaration of Human Rights: the right to an adequate standard of living. Our rights are universal, but not the allowances, not the money. If non-poor people have an adequate standard of living, do they have a right to more? If disabled people have major needs, should they not receive more? We have equal, universal rights precisely because we are all different and hence have different needs. Moreover, many needs should not be fulfilled with monetary allowances, but possibly with public services or other types of assistance. This is precisely what our systems of social assurances are for, based on a horizontal structural solidarity, from all according to means, to all according to needs. Universal social protection systems or welfare states, coupled to fair tax systems, are the progressive answer to social needs. With a basic income, giving the same amount to everyone, irrespective of income or resources, inequality remains unchanged.

Economic security is extremely important. Today it is threatened by new forms of precarity and informality in the labour market. However, it sounds rather cynical to me to accept this state of affairs and try to solve it with a basic income. What the workers' movement has done in the past is organise the struggle for decent wages and working conditions. Progressives can never be happy with the current state of affairs and the dismantlement of social and economic rights.

After the Second World War, the ILO (International Labour Organization) was able to issue its 'Declaration of Philadelphia'. In it, member states declared that 'labour is not a commodity'.[2] And indeed, thanks to social struggles and the then emerging welfare states, the power relations between labour and capital changed. Sure, the existence of the socialist threat in Eastern Europe helped. But there is no reason why we should accept the further weakening of rights and of workers' movements.

Moreover, if the basic income is not high enough for a decent way of living, people will still have to go out and work in the labour market. The basic income then becomes very rapidly a simple wage subsidy or an open door to 'mini jobs'. Surely, this is not a progressive solution.

Re-thinking social protection

Our social protection systems surely have to be adapted to the needs of people in the 21st century. We should not believe we can carry on as before. We should be able to re-think social protection, strengthen and broaden it, and most of all, involve all people and not just workers.

Let me start with the easy point on which we fully agree: social assistance needs fundamental changes. First of all, because poverty should not exist in our wealthy societies and because the current means testing and control mechanisms are humiliating and do not contribute to the empowerment of poor people. In spite of all academic and economic blah on the 'multidimensionality' of poverty, we should never forget that poor people need, in all market economies, an income if we want them to escape poverty. If other problems remain – health, education, housing, debt ... – after income security has been guaranteed, then social workers should be available to and ready to help.

A guaranteed minimum income for poor people should be introduced, urgently. This should indeed be an individual right. Since it would be for poor people only it does imply means testing, but this can easily be done without intervening in people's private lives. We have all the information technology available, from tax administration to social security, in order to grant people what they can rightly claim.

Why should we give a basic income to the non-poor? I have never heard a convincing argument. Non-poor people will pay it back through taxes, it is asserted. What can the rationale be for giving people money that they then have to give back? And more seriously, will the rich really pay back?

And finally, many advocates of basic income are now in favour of additional 'earnings-related social insurance'. Even social assistance cannot be expected to disappear, writes Van Parijs.

The 'basic income will not enable us to dispense with means-tested top ups for people in specific circumstances'.

The objectives of the basic income movement can be shared, but progressives will look for other solutions, based on solidarity, reciprocity and collective responsibility. Basic income is an individual solution that reduces the responsibility of public authorities and leaves people to care for themselves.

The advocates of basic income rightly point to the many problems we are faced with. But there is more than one answer and I do not think basic income is the best, since it depoliticises social protection. Nor is it the only possible solution.

Welfare states should urgently be re-thought, de-bureaucratised and democratised. The division between social security and social assistance should be abandoned, the dichotomy between re-productive and productive work should disappear. Our rights are individual and universal, whereas we should be able to also protect our societies. I want to plead for 'social commons', a democratic and participatory system in which people can become, once again, social and political actors, emancipated people who know what they are fighting for.[3]

Many bridges can be built between the basic income idea and social protection. The priority should be minimum incomes for the poor, decent pensions and family allowances, universal health care and quality education.

If people want to introduce a system to share the world's wealth, which also seems to be Van Parijs' objective, they can try to introduce the idea of a dividend. But this should not be seen as an alternative to social protection. It is a long-term utopia, which should not replace the urgent need and possibility to eradicate poverty.

A version of this article first appeared in the online journal, 'Social Europe' on 14 April 2016: socialeurope.eu/basic-income-can-never-progressive-solution.

Why basic income can never be a progressive solution

19

Basic income: a powerful tax engine pulling a tiny cart

Ian Gough, UK

'I fear that this latest plan will drain the energies of the
left in social policy and will divert attention from so
many other worthwhile policy alternatives.'

Yet another proposal for basic income, this time from the left.[4] It
is an evangelical, revolutionary idea (once hailed as 'the capitalist
road to communism') but it is deluded and diversionary. The
Compass scheme does set out how to pay for a partial basic
income for all: a rise in all income tax rates of 5p, the abolition
of the personal tax allowance and the extension of national
insurance contributions to all employees. These will raise the
bulk of the £210bn gross cost. What is achieved? A big cut in child
poverty, yes, but tiny falls in pensioner and working age adult
poverty, despite the latter being the basic goal of the policy. And
the numbers reliant on means testing will be cut by only one-fifth.

Thus a powerful new tax engine will pull along a tiny cart
(a partial and inadequate basic income). Why bother? The
underlying belief or dream is that basic income will provide a
mobilising theme to bring about radical change. There is no
evidence anywhere in the world for this. Similar proposals have

been made every few years for the last 50 years and they have got nowhere (and I do not mention Switzerland).

The problem is that it combines a radical vision with a naive or insouciant view of politics. Like all big-bang solutions it ignores contexts, politics and transitions. Somehow the fact that it is also advocated by neoliberals and Silicon Valley libertarians is seen as a plus.

I fear that this latest plan will drain the energies of the left in social policy and will divert attention from so many other worthwhile policy alternatives: the living wage, boosting trade unionism, free childcare, radical changes in housing policy, policies to reduce working time to limit turbo-consumption, green investment and so on.

Letter to the Guardian, 10 June 2016: theguardian.com/politics/2016/jun/10/potential-benefits-and-pitfalls-of-a-universal-basic-income

Basic income: a powerful tax engine pulling a tiny cart

20

A basic income and the democratisation of social policy

Peter Beresford OBE, UK

'... a basic income ... is essentially another social policy prescription that has developed top-down and been advanced by a relatively narrow body of 'experts''

The idea of a basic income has a long history, has attracted wide academic and political interest and currently feels like the 'next big thing' in social policy. Of course it has its doubters as well as its supporters and as many arguments have been offered against it by critics, as have been in its support by enthusiasts. For example, a Commission of the German Parliament concluded in 2013 that it was 'unrealizable', identifying an intimidating list of perceived deficiencies to back up its claim:

- It would cause a significant decrease in the motivation to work among citizens, with unforeseen consequences for the national economy.
- It would require a complete restructuring of the taxation, social insurance and pension systems, which would cost a significant amount of money.
- The current system of social help in Germany is regarded as more effective because it's more personalised: the amount

of help provided is not fixed and depends on the financial situation of the person; for some socially vulnerable groups the basic income could be not sufficient.
- It would cause a vast increase in immigration.
- It would cause a rise of the shadow economy.
- The corresponding rise of taxes would cause more inequality: higher taxes would translate themselves into higher prices of everyday products, harming the poor.
- No viable way to finance basic income in Germany was found.[5]

On the other hand, advocates of a basic income highlight how radical an innovation it is – a real break from the social policy past – and argue that it can surmount many of the weaknesses of traditional approaches to social security, notably means testing.[6]

What I want to explore in this article is neither the claims nor counter claims of advocates or opponents, rather I want to examine how far it represents a break from the dominant tradition of social policy and addresses the key concerns of those who have most challenged these: those people who experience social policy's heavy end and long-term effects. I begin by exploring the shortcoming of that dominant tradition before considering basic income in relation to them.

It is important to remember that in recent years constituencies long excluded from social policy discussions have begun to offer critical perspectives on all aspects of it – including initiatives like a basic income. Radical new insights about social policy were offered by the social movements emerging in the second half of the 20th century: the women's, black civil rights, LGBTQ and environmental movements followed by international movements of welfare service users from the last quarter of the 20th century.[7]

The first of these to emerge from the 1970s was the international disabled people's movement, swiftly followed by movements of mental health service users/survivors, people with learning difficulties, older people and people living with HIV/AIDS. They developed their own user-controlled organisations, services, arts, cultures, research, histories, theories and philosophies, and have given rise internationally to distinct areas of intellectual activity, notably disability studies and mad studies,[8] which now impact on mainstream academic learning and knowledge formation. These individual groups and movements have highlighted common issues and themes, including:

- challenging the prevailing medicalised individualistic understandings of them that underpin policy, and making the case instead for more social understandings which highlight the barriers and prejudices they face;
- highlighting that the poverty and disadvantage they face should be seen as part of broader discriminations and exclusions they experience;
- arguing the importance of being able to speak and act for themselves rather than being spoken for by other people and organisations;
- making claims to develop their own knowledge production and organisations rather than being the object of others' theories and charity/state intervention.[9]

Their understanding of their own situation has been most clearly summed up by the social model of disability and philosophy of independent living developed by the disabled people's movement. Both turn traditional disability thinking on its head. The social model of disability distinguishes between individual impairment or bodily loss and broader disabling barriers created in response to this, and explores the disabling/excluding effects of impairment. The philosophy of independent living rejects the traditional idea that disabled people are dependent because they need help, arguing that we all do and calls for policies and practices which offer disabled people the support they need to live *independently* on as equal terms as they can with non-disabled people. Instead of understanding their situation in terms of 'needs' that require a welfare response, they see it in terms of the denial of human and civil rights, requiring a *political* solution.[10]

As we might expect, such critiques from service user movements and theoreticians have been associated with the identification of major shortcomings in traditional social policy and welfare state

A basic income and the democratisation of social policy

systems. These arise from a process that is imposed on service users without their meaningful involvement, and dependent on the prescriptions of self-appointed experts.

They also make the case that social policies informed by neoliberal ideology which seek to reduce the support available to people have the same limitations because they are based on the same process.

This process which originates in late 19th century Fabian social policy has become the hallmark of almost all social policy thinking and practice. A group of self-appointed experts set out what they think should be done and seek its implementation. We have seen this right through the course of modern social policy, from the new poor law utilitarians, through the Beveridgean welfare staters, to the monetarists, proponents of new public management and neo-liberalism who have informed modern politicians from Margaret Thatcher through Tony Blair and Bill Clinton to Donald Trump. These have used populist approaches to promote such policy. The Fabians, however unsuccessful they have been in challenging neoliberal policymakers, have stood by their longstanding model of developing social policy. They base this on a process of what they see as:

- 'scientific' analysis
- production of evidence to inform and influence public policy
- the key role of 'expert' (themselves) in this social policy process.[11]

This process is meant to result in the education of the 'public' by these experts leading to the enactment of change. Unfortunately, in the UK at least, this model has not worked since Margaret Thatcher ignored such experts. But the model also has fundamental failings, as we can see from the post-war UK welfare state that was created on its basis.

First, it was paternalistic and reliant on one group of better-off people doing good to the rest of us. Right-wing politicians from Margaret Thatcher onwards ruthlessly exploited this weakness. Thatcher recognised that people did not like being bossed around, for example, by council landlords and forced, for instance, to have the same colour front doors. She injected a new consumerist rhetoric of involvement, choice and ownership which has carried popular conviction, even if her signature home ownership policy is a stark example of its failure.

Secondly, the welfare state failed to marry diversity with equality, so that, for example, its notion of 'full employment' penalised women and marginalised disabled people. Given that the welfare state, for all its altruistic goals, was the creation of, essentially, a group of white upper middle class able-bodied men, this was hardly surprising.

Now let me return to the idea of a basic income. Whatever its merits, it is essentially another social policy prescription developed top-down and advanced by a relatively narrow body of 'experts'. Like predecessors, it has come in for criticism from some feminists and disabled people and even now these issues are not being addressed adequately (for example, the costs of disability). I consider this the most important issue its advocates need to resolve. Can they transform it from being another bright idea from above to one that has involved, engaged and drawn on the diversity of people it is meant to benefit? Can they enable it to make the move from paternalism to participation? Can it achieve broad ownership, instead of just being one of a long list of imposed expert nostrums?

Hopefully such a process of democratising the idea and its development could also deal with other troubling issues. We know, for example, from social policy internationally, that ideas which have been developed with progressive intentions can end up being regressive and unhelpful when implemented. Well-known examples in the UK include, for instance, high rise council housing estates, which ended up being seen as ghettoes and demolished, and Blairite tax credit schemes that perpetuated low wages and low grade employment. How do we avoid prescriptions like a basic income being diluted by policymakers, especially when we know that support for them has come from very different quarters, including some right-wing thinkers whose preoccupation is with reducing state support? In recent years we

A basic income and the democratisation of social policy

have even seen the grassroots proposals of service users and their organisations, like direct payments, peer support and 'recovery' subverted through the nature of their implementation.[12]

An even bigger issue associated with basic income is that interest in it has been linked with concerns about the feasibility of a traditional labour market in the light of modern economic and technical developments. The logic of globalised capitalist economies is to seek reductions in employment costs and increased automation. What jobs will there be for people in the future? Won't there have to be an alternative source of income? It is ironic that in advanced economies like the UK and the US, people seem to be working longer hours than ever. There is a danger in the promotion of a basic income as a new idea of forgetting that it may rest on capitalist premises.

There is also a need to develop economies consistent with sustainability and the protection of the environment. But this ignores the fact that there will still be very many jobs to be done – jobs that can be more flexible and accessible (even if there may be some people for whom employment is not a reasonable option) if we are committed to a world and societies based on mutuality, social justice and equal opportunity. These are exactly the kind of jobs that have been cut most determinedly under neoliberal economies: public sector jobs concerned with how we look after each other through education, health and care; taking care of our neighbourhoods, arts and recreation; public transport, our heritage and history; and planning for the future. In a progressive society the jobs thus generated will need to be coupled with opportunities and decent conditions.[13]

So my suggestion is that if we really want to give the idea of a basic income a fair chance, we need to think more about how we can democratise the discussion and process – and about what its economic, political, social and cultural contexts are. Most ideas are neutral; it's what we do with them that determines how helpful they become. We now have a chance to maximise the value of this particular one – a basic income for all.

21

Why a basic income is not good enough

Ed Whitfield, USA

'This is why I oppose guaranteed income: "... the one who feeds you usually imposes his will upon you." We have enough of that already.'

I've spent a lot of time lately speaking against the establishment of a guaranteed minimum income. I want to make a few things clear to those who think I don't care about meeting needs:

1. I feel the current distribution of wealth is grotesquely unfair.
2. I don't believe that those who cannot or will not work should be allowed to starve.
3. I would be against plans to eliminate or cut the existing welfare system as long as it is needed.
4. I believe that we should build a community in which everyone's needs are met.

But, even so, I oppose fighting for a guaranteed income. Let me explain why.

Looked at closely, guaranteed basic income is simply more widely available welfare. It would only help people have more access to consumption without altering anything about how production is organised. It would not alter wealth distribution and ownership. And finally, it would require a new bureaucracy staffed by agents and experts to regulate and allocate this universal distribution of money.

My objections have surprised many people, but I think they are consistent with what I do think is the solution to our economic justice problem. I favour deep democracy replacing the rule of capital in our lives. This would require reparations and the reconstruction of the commons, but this time including the earth and the fungible financial resources that have been created by our labour within exploiting systems.

Our economy suffers from the fact that communities are not having their needs met and the quality of life equitably elevated for all. Neither the self-regulated market nor the intervention of government has been successful in doing this to the satisfaction of the many. The lack of purchasing power of working class people is a factor in the cyclical crises we face. The few who are privileged within and dominate the existing system induce others to believe that, rather than oppose their domination and exploitation, we should instead struggle to emulate the rich and then all of who are worthy could be successful and take care of our responsibility to others. We are also told not to bother to understand how we got into the situation we are in, but rather to forget the past and look ahead to the future.

Reparations and the cow

Those who argue the loudest for letting the past go are those who continue to benefit from the disparity. Their call to forget the past is a call to allow them to retain their unearned privilege, pretending that they deserve it.

I'm reminded of a story that I was told by Reverend Bugani Finca who was involved in South Africa's Truth and Reconciliation work. A black South African, Tabo, confronted a white man, Mr Smith, who had disrespected him and stolen his prize cow. With the prospect of amnesty for telling the truth, the white man admitted to having done what he was accused of, recognised how horribly wrong it was and asked for forgiveness, saying that he was truly sorry. Tabo was visibly relieved for having an opportunity to confront his oppressor and get an apology. They shook hands and embraced. As Mr Smith stood to leave, free, with his amnesty, the black man called out to stop him. The white man turned back with a questioning look on his face, not sure why he was being stopped. Tabo asked him: 'But what about the cow?' Mr Smith was visibly angry: 'You are ruining our reconciliation', he shouted, 'This has nothing to do with a cow.'

That is the question we must ask to all those who say that the past is long gone but still retain ownership of the herd produced by that old cow. We won't forgive and forget until we get the cow back. But just suppose that the Mr Smiths in the world make a counter offer: 'I'll tell you what, why don't I just give you a supply of butter?' 'The hell', Tabo might reply, 'If you give me back my cow, I can give you butter!'

Guaranteed income is a supply of butter. More than that, it makes two assumptions, both of which I think are false: it assumes that the government can simply pay out the money without having other negative consequences for the economy as a whole, and it also assumes that there is a rational amount of money and process for its allocation that experts can figure out and apply fairly.

What I believe to be true is that with labour being the sole creator of value, there is no place for the money to come from but out of the social surplus, either as taxes or reduced wages. There is a political and economic price to be paid that cannot be avoided. I also have a healthy distrust for decision making by experts. Typically, in spite of their declarations and the veneer of objectivity, they are guided by the class interests of those deeply entrenched in, and benefitting from, the status quo. I have never heard that there would be a deeply democratic regulatory process to work out the details of a guaranteed income. As one of those intimately involved in the attempts to implement trials in the United States 40 years ago has shown, it was hard to make such a scheme work.[14]

What I do think we need is reparations, the democratisation of wealth, the recreation of the commons and the outlawing of theft and speculation. I think that communities must become

Why a basic income is not good enough

their own developers through broadly democratic planning any democratic access to non-extractive financing. The details of how these things are done is the content of many more pieces. But the key is democracy and expanded opportunities to be productive rather than enhanced consumption. We need the cow back, not just a supply of butter.

Finally, I want to say that even though some conservative economists and politicians have found guaranteed income to be something that they support, there is widespread opposition and a serious political struggle would need to be mounted to attain that end. I would hate to see us squander that much of our energy, resources and time on what would objectively be a giant welfare system.

Dara Cooper, a good friend of mine, ended an email to me with this quote about the impact of foreign aid from Thomas Sankara, former President of Burkina Fasa, assassinated in 1987:

> 'We can even produce more than we need. Unfortunately, because of lack of organization, we still need to beg for food aid and this has kept us thinking that we can only be beggars who need aid. We must produce more because the one who feeds you usually imposes his will upon you.'

This is why I oppose guaranteed income: '... the one who feeds you usually imposes his will upon you.' We have enough of that already.

22

Unconditional basic income is a dead end

Anke Hassel, Germany

'... basic income ... benefits the margins of society at the expense of the middle class. For the poor and long-term unemployed, the basic income removes the pressure to find work and the unpleasant task of motivating people to actively look for employment. It most likely won't cost the rich any more than before, and helps ease their social conscience.'

The concept of an unconditional basic income is becoming increasingly popular among economists, managers, activists and entrepreneurs as an alternative to traditional social policy. Instead of providing social benefits in an emergency, for unemployment or old age, the government would pay every adult the same lump sum in the future - around €1,000–1,200 a month. There would then be no social benefits, no Hartz IV (Germany's long-term jobless benefits), and most likely no pension or unemployment insurance.

This universal basic income promises each person the freedom to decide if they want to be employed, to do volunteer work - or do nothing at all. It promises politicians the luxury of no longer worrying about unemployment. And it gives companies an elegant way to justify job cuts. Jobs that fall victim to technological change or globalisation are no longer a problem, as those affected are financially secure and can look after their children at home or pursue hobbies.

Nevertheless, the basic income is a dead end. The most commonly cited reason for this is, of course, financing. Its costs have not been quantified, but it is certain that they will be high. Just how income and wealth should be taxed to pay for it remains an open question. Radically transforming the social system to a basic income would be the greatest financial gamble in recent history.

But the financial aspect is not even the most important argument against a basic income. The basic income is a seductive poison. It benefits the margins of society at the expense of the middle class. For the poor and long-term unemployed, the basic income removes the pressure to find work and the unpleasant task of motivating people to actively look for employment. It most likely won't cost the rich any more than before, and helps ease their social conscience. In this case, growing social inequality would no longer be a social scandal, since everyone would have an income, albeit close to the poverty line. It is precisely for this reason that there are three main arguments against an unconditional basic income.

First, the basic income will further divide society and prevent social mobility. Those who, due to their family background, have good prospects for interesting employment and high income will maintain their existing work ethic, engaging in school and study, and maybe taking a sabbatical or two in between. This is a good thing. However, life will become more difficult for young people from parts of society already at a disadvantage in terms of education – those from working class and migrant families. The sweet poison of the basic income will accompany them in every step of their school life and vocational training. When asked what they want to do for a living, children from parts of Berlin with a high percentage of working class and migrant families, such as Neuköln, today already often say they plan to go on the dole. In the future, they will answer: 'I'll get my basic income.' Their numbers will rise as the basic income rises. Their motivation to continue to invest in themselves and to improve their lives through qualified work will be put to the test every day and at an age when they are already struggling with themselves and the demands of their environment. The rest of society will be much less concerned about this development than they are today, as everyone will be taken care of.

Second, an unconditional basic income lacks social legitimacy. At present, it is impossible to imagine a model that benefits all parts of society equally. It is therefore likely that the basic income would be redistributed from the centre of society to those who are not, or are only partially, employed. Comprehensive social services that go beyond pure poverty control, however, are legitimised by existing concepts of social justice. How else? Norms of social justice include the idea of equal opportunity, giving everyone a shot at making it on the labour market and in the market place. This justifies, for instance, public spending on education or inheritance tax. Or the idea of social insurance which links contribution for unemployment and old age insurance to social transfers.

An unconditional basic income is, in principle, based on a citizen's right to income, although it leaves open the question as to why it should also be paid to those who do not need it. Social solidarity with the weaker members of society is the opposite of a basic income scheme. The middle class, who would finance the basic income but who wouldn't benefit from it materially, are unlikely to find social justice in this 'unconditional' redistribution. This is why large redistribution programmes are unpopular among voters, even among those who are likely to benefit from it. For this reason, in a 2016 referendum, the Swiss rejected by a large majority the proposal to introduce a basic income.

Third, an unconditional basic income runs counter to the needs of a society with rapidly growing immigration. A large number of migrant workers and other immigrants need more mechanisms to help with social integration, not fewer. It's the everyday experiences that matter: people meet each other at work, they get to know and appreciate each other, and they learn the language. Considering this, it would be fatal to give people a reason to stop working, to stop improving their qualifications, and to simply stay at home. Nevertheless, we need a debate about a good society that is not based solely on employment and the labour market. There is still a lot of work necessary to improve society that cannot be accomplished through the labour market, but that still needs to be acknowledged. But the unconditional basic income is the wrong way to accomplish this.

This piece originally appeared in a blog for the Hertie School of Governance, Berlin, on 23 February 2017; hertie-school.org/en/debate/opinion/detail/content/the-unconditional-basic-income-is-a-dead-end/

Unconditional basic income is a dead end

PART IV: BUILDING FOR CHANGE

23

Basic income and social democracy*

Philippe Van Parijs, Belgium

'As regards social protection, [we must make] room for
a third model fundamentally different both from the old
social assistance model – public charity – and from the
social insurance model – worker solidarity – with which
social democracy has been closely associated and which
it feels it is its duty to defend.'

The idea of an unconditional basic income is in fashion. From
Finland to Switzerland, from San Francisco to Seoul, people talk
about it as they have never done. Twice before, basic income
was the object of a real public debate, albeit briefly and limited
to one country at a time. In both episodes, the centre left played
a central role.

The first debate took place in England in the aftermath of
World War I. The Quaker and engineer Dennis Milner managed
to get his 'state bonus' proposal discussed at the 1920 Labour
Party conference. It was rejected, but prominent members of the
party kept defending it in the following years under the label
'social dividend'. Among them were the Oxford economist and
political theorist George Cole and the future Nobel laureate
James Meade.[1]

The second debate took place in the United States in the late
1960s and early 1970s. Another future Nobel laureate, James
Tobin, advocated the introduction of a 'demogrant', along with

Harvard economist and best-selling author John Kenneth Galbraith, also on the left of the Democratic Party. Persuaded by them, Senator George McGovern included the proposal in his programme during his campaign for the nomination as democratic presidential candidate, but dropped it in the last months before the 1972 presidential election, which he lost to Richard Nixon.

The current, far longer and increasingly global debate originates in Europe in the 1980s. Interest for basic income arose more or less simultaneously in several countries and prompted the creation of a network (BIEN) that now has national branches in all continents. This time, however, the social democratic left is not exactly at the forefront, far less than the greens, for example, or than some components of the liberal right and the far left.

What is there in basic income that can trigger the suspicion of social democrats and what is there in it that should prompt its enthusiasm? In order to answer such questions, it is important to clarify what a basic income is and what it is not.

A basic income is an income that is unconditional in three senses in which existing minimum income schemes are also unconditional: it is paid in cash, entitlement is not conditional on having paid social security contributions, and it is not restricted to citizens. It is also unconditional in three additional senses. It is *individual*, i.e. independent of its beneficiaries' household situation. It is *universal*, i.e. entitlement to it is not dependent on the level of their income from other sources. And it is *duty-free*, i.e. not restricted to those working or willing to work.

Is it not absurd to pay such a basic income to all, including the rich? It is not. The absence of an income test is not better for the rich. It is better for the poor. True, the rich do not need a basic income, just as they do not need to have the lowest layers of their incomes untaxed or taxed at low rates, as they do under current personal income tax systems. High earners will of course pay for their own basic income and for part of the basic incomes paid to others. One great advantage of an income paid automatically to all, irrespective of income, is that it reaches the poor far more effectively than a means-tested scheme, and without stigmatisation. Another is that it provides them with a floor on which they can stand, because it can be combined with earnings, rather than a net in which they can easily get stuck because it is withdrawn if poor people start earning.

Is it not unacceptable to replace the right to a job by a right to an income? A basic income does nothing of the sort. On the contrary. It provides a flexible, intelligent form of job sharing. It makes it easier for people who work too much to reduce their working time or take a career break. It enables the jobless to pick up the employment thereby freed, the more easily as they can do so on a part-time basis, since their earnings are being added to their basic income. And the firm floor provided by the basic income makes for a more fluid back and forth between employment, training and family that should reduce the occurrence of burnout and early retirement, thus enabling people to spread employment over a longer portion of their lives. As social democrats rightly emphasise, access to paid work is important for reasons over and above the income it provides. Those who advocate a basic income paid without a work condition do not need to deny this. It is even taken for granted by those who are confident that a generous unconditional basic income is sustainable: despite a less miserable fall-back option and higher taxation, people will keep working precisely because work means far more to them than just an income.

Does the introduction of a basic income not threaten the very existence of our welfare states? On the contrary, it comes to their rescue. Needless to say, a basic income is by no means an alternative to publicly funded education and health care. Nor is it meant to provide a full substitute to earnings-related social insurance benefits funded by workers' social contributions. Given that each household member will have his or her basic income, however, the levels of the cash benefits and the funding they require can be correspondingly reduced, the benefits individualised and simplified, and the depth of the traps associated with the conditions to which they are subjected will shrink.

Even in the longer run, social assistance cannot be expected to disappear either. Because of its being both individual and universal, sensible levels of basic income will not enable us to dispense with means-tested top ups for people in specific circumstances. Again, given the unconditional floor, traps will be reduced, the number of people dependent on these conditional benefits will shrink and the social workers' important job will be facilitated. Fitting an unconditional floor under the existing welfare state will not dismantle but strengthen our duly readjusted social insurance and social assistance schemes.

It is nonetheless true that a basic income constitutes a model of social protection fundamentally different from these existing two models. Consequently, one can expect people most closely involved in the pre-existing system to feel challenged and to oppose resistance. This was the case in the early 16th century when municipal public assistance challenged the monopoly of Church-organised charity, and from the late 19th century when state-organised pension and health insurance systems challenged the position of poor relief institutions. It is not far-fetched to conjecture that the lack of enthusiasm for basic income among social democrats and in labour organisations has something to do with the important role they have been playing in initiating, developing and managing the social insurance schemes that now form the bulk of most of our welfare states.

Such resistance is perfectly understandable, indeed laudable: our social-insurance-based welfare states make a huge difference in terms of social justice and are therefore well worth defending. But this does not exempt social democrats from urgently updating their doctrine in order to better address the demands of our century: a century in which both the desirability and possibility of indefinite growth have lost for good the obviousness social democrats were banking on in the previous century, a century in which full-time life-long waged labour will only be possible and desirable for a minority, a century in which the left cannot let the right monopolise the theme of freedom.

As regards social protection, this requires making room for a third model fundamentally different both from the old social assistance model – public charity – and from the social insurance model – worker solidarity – with which social democracy has been closely associated and which it feels is its duty to defend. In order to be able to address today's challenges, the left will need to move from 'labourism' to 'socialism', as it were, by getting rid of an illusion which has been at the core of much left-wing thinking ever since Marx's theory of exploitation. It needs to recognise fully that the bulk of our real incomes is not the fruit of the efforts of today's workers (let alone of the abstinence of today's capitalists), but a gift from nature increasingly combined with capital accumulation, technological innovation and institutional improvements inherited from the past. In a 'labourist' perspective, those morally entitled to this gift – whether directly in the form of wages or indirectly in the form of social benefits to which they are entitled through their work – are the present generation of workers, in proportion to the market value of their skills, the length of their working time and their bargaining power. In a truly 'socialist' perspective, those entitled to this gift are all members of society.

This more egalitarian, more emancipatory, less male-biased perspective entails a strong presumption in favour of an unconditional basic income. It is not something the left should be dreading. It is something it should enthusiastically embrace.[2]

This piece was originally published in 'Social Europe', 11 April 2016; socialeurope.eu/44878

*See Chapter 18 for a response to this chapter.

24

History and the contemporary debate in the UK

Malcolm Torry, Citizen's Basic Income Trust, UK

'It is not impossible that unforeseen circumstances might result in the UK being the first country to implement a genuine citizen's basic income and reaping the rewards that will accrue to an early mover. But the UK is not at its most innovative at the moment, and it is perfectly possible that Namibia, India, or some other country, will implement a scheme long before the UK gets round to it.'

The importance of definition

A citizen's basic income is an unconditional, automatic and non-withdrawable payment to each individual as a right of citizenship. It has other names: basic income, universal basic income, citizen's income – but it's always the same thing.

- **Unconditional**: A citizen's income would vary with age, but there would be no other conditions: so everyone of the same age would receive the same payment, whatever their gender, employment status, family structure, contribution to society, housing costs, or anything else.

- **Automatic**: Someone's citizen's income would be paid weekly or monthly, automatically.
- **Non-withdrawable**: Citizen's incomes would not be means-tested. If someone's earnings or wealth increased, then their citizen's income would not change.
- **Individual**: Citizen's incomes would be paid on an individual basis, and not on the basis of a couple or household.
- **As a right of citizenship**: Everybody legally resident in the UK would receive a citizen's income, subject to a minimum period of legal residency in the UK, and continuing residency for most of the year.

It is essential to be clear about this definition. One of the results of the increasingly lively global debate is that terminology has proliferated, and so has its meanings. In the United States and in Canada 'basic income' sometimes means an income-tested benefit, and it can also mean one that varies with household structure. 'Citizen's income' or 'citizen's basic income' always means an unconditional, automatic and non-withdrawable payment to each individual.

The history of the debate in the UK

The two late 18th century advocates of citizen's basic income, Thomas Paine and Thomas Spence, were British (although by the time he was writing about the idea Paine was living in the United States);[3] and since then the idea has occasionally emerged into public debate and then as quickly disappeared. During the early 20th century, the State Bonus League campaigned for a citizen's basic income, or 'state bonus'; and in 1921 the Labour Party Executive Committee discussed the idea and rejected it.[4]

In 1943, Lady Juliet Rhys Williams, a member of the Beveridge Committee, published *Something to Look Forward To*,[5] which suggested something like a citizen's basic income, but the Beveridge system of national insurance prevailed; and in 1982 her son, Brandon Rhys Williams, a Conservative Member of Parliament, recommended a citizen's basic income to a select committee.[6] This proposed that 'the Government should put ... work in hand'.[7] A general election followed, and nothing was done. The one exception to this pattern is the Family Allowance Act, passed by the UK Parliament in 1945, which granted unconditional payments for the second and subsequent children of every family:[8] the closest we've ever got to a citizen's basic income in the UK.

In 1984 a group of individuals formed the Basic Income Research Group (later renamed the 'Citizen's Income Trust', and now the 'Citizen's Basic Income Trust'), and since then the Trust has promoted debate, published a regular newsletter, organised meetings, maintained a library and a website, responded to requests for information, and submitted evidence to parliamentary enquiries.

For the next 30 years not a lot changed. No major newspaper carried an article on the subject; other media showed no interest; and in the academic and policymaking worlds, citizen's basic income was regarded as a fringe interest with no practical relevance. And then about four years ago things began to change.

In 2014, Larry Elliott, the economics editor of the *Guardian*, read my *Money for Everyone*[9] and wrote an article and since then there have been numerous articles on citizen's basic income in mainstream newspapers and journals. The news in 2016 – premature as it turned out – that Finland was about to implement a scheme led to television and radio interviews, an entire Radio 4 'Money Box Live' programme (on 13 January 2016), and requests for radio and television interviews continue. The European Citizen's Initiative on Basic Income, launched in 2013 as part of a European Union initiative to encourage citizens to participate directly in its development, gave birth to new organisations with a more campaigning character (in the UK, Basic Income UK was formed, and works closely with Citizen's Basic Income Trust, the former concentrating on campaigning, and the latter on more educational activity – although the line between these two activities is of course somewhat hazy).

The significant results from the 2009 Namibia Citizen's Basic Income pilot project have been reinforced by those from the larger 2009–13 Indian project (see Chapter 26), and although the experiment in Finland is in some respects not strictly about a citizen's basic income, the launch of experiments of various kinds continues to drive interest (see Part V). And then there have been an increasing number of reports and books published, most recently by the Royal Society of Arts, Compass, Guy Standing, Philippe Van Parijs, Annie Miller, and myself.[10]

This describes *what* has happened in the UK, but not entirely *why* it has happened. I have heard many suggestions as to the reasons for the increasing interest in citizen's basic income among politicians, academics, and to some extent the general public. A frequent suggestion is that we are becoming increasingly aware that automation and globalisation might make employment a decreasingly secure route to an income. In response, one has to say that it is impossible to make confident predictions about how the employment market will change in the future, but the anxiety about some of the possibilities does appear to be driving some of the increasing interest. Similarly, we are increasingly aware of growing poverty and inequality levels, and citizen's basic income is sometimes offered as a solution: but again one has to say that a citizen's basic income scheme would not necessarily reduce poverty and inequality, although there are of course illustrative schemes that would do so[11] (see Chapters 29 and 30). We are also increasingly aware that means-tested benefits function as a significant employment disincentive because they are withdrawn as earnings rise: and in relation to this problem we *can* confidently predict that a citizen's basic income would contribute to a solution.

At least as significant as the increasing level of debate is the way in which the debate has changed. Until about five years ago it was purely about whether a citizen's basic income was a good idea: so it was compared with means-tested and national insurance benefits, and their relative advantages and disadvantages were discussed. But by 2014 the academic world was becoming more interested in the question of feasibility (one symptom of which was that I was asked to write a book about *The Feasibility of Citizen's Income*[12]). We have now seen a further shift in the debate: towards questions of implementation – a symptom of which was the Institute of Chartered Accountants in England and Wales' consultation in 2016 on options for implementing a citizen's basic income.[13]

What will happen next? Whether the debate will continue to increase in depth and breadth, or whether it will subside, as it frequently has before, nobody can know. Similarly, nobody can know how political debate on the subject will evolve. Both the UK's 1945 Family Allowance Act, and its extension to the first child in the family 30 years later, could be described as political accidents, as could Iran's implementation of something like a citizen's basic income.[14] It is not impossible that unforeseen circumstances might result in the UK being the first country to implement a genuine citizen's basic income and reaping the rewards that will accrue to an early mover. But the UK is not at its most innovative at the moment, and it is perfectly possible that Namibia, India, or some other country will implement a scheme long before the UK gets round to it.

All we can promise is that the Citizen's Basic Income Trust will continue to promote debate by maintaining a website, by undertaking and publishing research, and by responding to requests for information; and Basic Income UK will continue to campaign. We shall, as always, respond to the way in which the debate is changing, as no doubt it will continue to do; and we shall also of course continue to work for the integrity of the debate's terminology, and in particular to ensure that 'citizen's basic income' always means an unconditional, automatic and non-withdrawable regular payment for every individual.

History and the contemporary debate in the UK

25

Basic income and the democratisation of development in Europe

Louise Haagh, UK

'All that is needed is a change of mind-set, so that it can become accepted that basic income is a form of universal security like public education and health.'

In this chapter I discuss how the proposal for basic income (BI) – a subsistence grant paid regularly and permanently, or for life, to every resident of a given political territory – is a humanist and democratic reform, and as such not necessarily radical. Many contemporary arguments set up the case for basic income as an alternative to systems we know, to make the case more compelling. One such narrative is the idea that BI is a radical replacement of the welfare state. For instance, basic income has been classically presented as a freedom-orientated alternative to ways social democracy seeks to transform (control) man and promote consumption.[15] More recent arguments situate basic income as a source to reinvent the capitalist system, by promoting self-help, a smoothing of consumption, or a form of adaptation to displacement of socially organised work by forces of automation. A version of the portrayal of basic income as a systemic shift towards self-organising society has been presented recently by the founder of Facebook, Mark Zuckerberg,[16] when he argued basic income on a mode of Alaska's resources dividend offers a form of alternative welfare, and a smaller state.[17]

The problem with Zuckerberg's vision – as well as with the portrayal of basic income as an alternative to social democracy – is that a too polarised view of the role of the state and of public versus private ownership is entailed. Zuckerberg mentions state support of private fishing in Alaska as an example of a way smaller government can support self-help.[18] But if state support of fishing stock may be a good example of state development policy this does not make development policy an alternative to universal welfare or to regulatory approaches to promote rights in formal employment. Historically, public ownership and a strong fiscal nexus has been the background for combining these forms of public policy in continental European welfare states.

The challenge of basic income today is to enable collective forms of governing on a new basis, not as the role of the state is non-constitutive of freedom, but rather the opposite: as the weakening of state development policy has led the state to adopt an increasingly market-disciplinary approach to the problem of welfare and poverty.[19]

Hence, I suggest a better narrative for basic income – than as a displacement of public ownership in the delivery of welfare – is one focused on reconstituting humanist governance from the ground up, an element in a wider challenge to re-democratise the state. To make this case, I have argued commitments to something very similar to a basic income were made in Europe after the Second World War in the context of consolidation and extension of universal public health and schooling.[20] We should be asking not why we should have a basic income but why we do not have it.

Likely reasons basic income did not become part of modern welfare structures include the incremental and often uncoordinated way income, tax, and social transfer systems developed. Added to this is the misconception that some proponents of basic income have contributed by suggesting a basic income would replace other unconditional transfers, contributory systems or needs-based services, as distinct from being – as one might also argue – simply the foundation for a more complex cooperative structure. In addition to this is the way the word 'income' is confusing. Many people assume all income is earnings.[21] But in fact it is not really: we receive many public goods that have or could have monetary value through services. There is no implication a basic income replaces opportunities or incentives to earn.

The recording of 'development' and contribution through the GDP statistic, comprising those things that are traded on the formal market, has surreptitiously come to be understood not as what it is – merely a form of accounting[22] – but as equal to social worth. If only things that are traded on the formal market have value, it means that there is no social worth to someone living modestly, and looking after themselves or their relatives, even if those behaviours are less costly than many that go on within the rubric of the GDP statistic.

So, simple conceptual errors made us not do something that would have been perfectly rational – to extend a legal guarantee of basic money security in a monetary economy. Had we done that it is conceivable that we could have averted many political and economic problems becoming crises. This is true in the case of the individual economy, as in present welfare state set-ups, crises like illness and unemployment become a person's condition when such events turn into reasons for disaffiliation from occupation and a source of a new state of controlled dependence. It is also true in national and global economies, where cooperative and political conflicts escalate when cooperative institutions and relations must break for the market economy to maintain equilibrium in the face of shock. This is the sort of risk that the economist Albert Hirschman wanted to insure against when thinking of mechanisms that would avoid too many institutions failing through competition, and support individuals' choice (exit), their affiliation to institutions (loyalty), and their say (voice).[23]

If not creating a real structure of independent security within the welfare state was a mistake, it is important to correct that now. We have corroded the commitment we still entertain to basic security by governing it through a sanctions regime that does the opposite of what we do in education and in health services. In turn this causes contradictions within our systems of governance. In countries like Britain and Denmark (see Chapter 17), about one in four persons on job-seekers' income support receive a sanction at some stage, where 15 years ago such measures were milder and much more rare.[24]

What has occurred in the progressive tightening of sanctions regimes in Europe needs to be seen in conjunction with the dilution of institutional incentives in the labour market, as free education access and employment protections and rights have weakened. In this context, it is factually misleading to ascribe the weakening of incentives to individuals and morally wrong to punish them for the outcome.

In a paper published in 2011 I argued that basic income is compatible with social democracy.[25] There are many reasons for this. Among them I pointed out how institutions of social democracy have helped raise individuals' control over time, a key objective and potential contribution of basic income reform, albeit one that relies on other regulatory policies to constitute real equality in social relations. Work-time reduction, quality public childcare, labour market institutions that police the size of workload and competition at work, and policies to promote gender equality in care and work, all intend to give individuals greater command of their daily lives and social relations.

Another reason basic income is compatible with social democracy is that Nordic states in different degrees have come very close, in practice, to providing unconditional security along lines that mimic what a basic income would do. In the 1980s and into the 1990s, the public expectation that working-age individuals were available for employment was loosely interpreted. I experienced this as a young person growing up in Denmark, but I am not alone in this perception.[26] The interpretation of contribution and cooperation as voluntary acts has a long tradition in the popular conception of democracy and rights that is the real source of the social democratic tradition. Regulatory interventions to reduce competition and promote

Basic income and the democratisation of development in Europe cooperative learning in public schooling are just some examples of this.[27] It is not that citizens are not expected to contribute in Nordic states, but that investment in institutions that would make the voluntary nature of contribution likely has historically been strong.

Since the 1990s – and especially since the mid-2000s – conditionalities and sanctions on the unemployed have grown in Nordic states, as in other countries. This is a reversal of the democratic tradition.[28] But the justification for sanctions is being questioned all over Europe, and not least in the Nordic states. The growing and quite practical support for basic income in Nordic states – demonstrated by in the Finnish government experiment, and several related local pilots to lift conditionalities by Danish municipalities (see Chapter 17) – bears out the general gist of the argument I made in 2011.

We need to ask not why we should have a basic income or what will happen if we have one, but what will happen if we do not. The governance failure that the sanctions regime represents is an indication of a crisis in public policy which we might call a policy stalemate.

A policy stalemate is where you cannot implement an effective policy because the institutions required to do so are in crisis or do not exist. When that happens, government becomes passive, or starts to turn on itself, because simply cutting things is at least one way of doing something. The inability to raise social contributions in Britain within the growing self-employed sector of work is an example of a policy stalemate. It is the kind of stalemate that a basic income could help resolve, because if people could achieve basic financial stability, then contributory savings within the economy that are important sources of affiliation, and of enabling public policy, may be imagined.

It is worth noting that the public economist, the late Tony Atkinson, who did envisage something like this, was led to argue against unconditional basic income because – it seems – he felt the case for combining BI and contribution had not been made strongly enough.[29]

For anyone who thinks development is a collective and public challenge, and that a developmental framing of work, research and investment is important and as such cannot be left to market players, a basic income is only a small element in re-civilising governance. But it is arguably an elementary step in a progressive agenda. It is important to set the tone for what is valuable, and as such what our public policies and shared institutions ought to protect.

One of the key ways a basic income might change current systems from within is that it represents a permanent form of stability, and it signals economic stability as a value. This is a significant shift in thinking. Even re-reading Hirschman, who was a progressive political economist for his time, it is notable how he never really questioned that the object of economic life was simply to enable market mechanisms to improve products ('consumers always know best').[30] Today no one really believes – not even American progressive liberals (such as Cass Sunstein) – that consumers always know best, because consumers do not have full knowledge.[31] The value of economic stability in this context is not stagnation, but economies evolving at a pace that is developmentally rational, and a form of public sphere that enables deliberation about development choices. Economic stability as a value may also help us reflect on how we integrate the different roles we play, as citizens, consumers, producers and carers, in society. The economy ultimately is made up of developmental trajectories within human lives. When economic processes in the economy break those trajectories, when the institutions that govern society are not designed to protect their integrity, there are both economic and social costs to society. Some of the ways in which the pace of competition breaks developmental trajectories are hidden within ostensibly protected spheres, like stable employment, where pressures to compete and retain positions on a constant basis induce stress, and the kinds of career inequalities known to affect women especially.

Basic income does not itself regenerate the formal occupational trajectories that many have reason to feel are needed within health and social care, conservation and green technologies. But basic income does create a basis to renegotiate work from within systems as they are today. If forces that have traditionally safeguarded human rights within the economy, such as labour unions, have been sceptical about basic income, that is understandable given the ways the argument has been made. However, many of the concerns labour unions have about basic income are based on bad arguments for basic income, not on good reason to think that securing a right to subsistence is against interests unions represent. What is the alternative? A regime that sanctions persons for not presenting in the labour market? It is hard to see how this is something a labour union should defend. Labour unions are right to enter the debate about basic income, and how it may be made to not stand in conflict with employment or other welfare rights. But basic income is a right to economic security: this means it strengthens the value of economic security rights. If I were a union representative I would suggest basic income can be a basis for negotiating more lasting and stable affiliations – even if people take a break – so that places of employment can become occupational affiliations in a new, more gender-equal way.[32]

Europe is confronting processes of informalisation of areas of the economy that present a danger for freedom and democracy. Informalisation ultimately will lead Europe to adopt the more behaviour-controlling forms of governing that are entailed when targeted anti-poverty policies come to dominate social policy.

In the 1990s, in Brazil, the argument was developed that basic income was a rational extension of anti-poverty policy cash grants.[33] As a student at the time of this process, I observed the amount of effort that went into identifying poor households, in some cases with lists that contained 40 different measurements of anything from whether you had a fridge to a fan. I observed how implausible this effort to be precisely fair was, in a context in which incomes within the household were fluctuating. The effort created evasion: stories were told of individuals moving furniture and livestock between houses on inspection day. The greater the poverty, the higher the stakes in exclusions, and the greater the new social tensions and stigma created.

The case of the Brazilian experience is relevant to Europe today. Why? It is relevant because a process of legal and economic informalisation is slowly emerging. Much has been written about how this has come from changes in the capitalist system, leading to precarious forms of contracting. Less has been said about how informalisation is an outcome of state policy, not only as a significant bulk of precarious contracting is within state-funded services, but as states are seeking to remove individuals from the public assistance case load.[34] The objective of doing so is tied to individual budget cut targets. However, the outcome in terms of destabilising social relations – through the phenomenon of non-wage non-dependence, and leaving persons unaccounted for – can be predicted to undermine efficacious public policy in the future in some of the ways I observed in Brazil.

Of course the debate about basic income intersects with a wider debate about the value of public goods and finance. But the relationship is not the way is has been standardly presented. Classic arguments for basic income have spent too much analytical energy trying to present how basic income is an alternative to socialised welfare, when the institutions and values that will fund and govern a basic income are those that created the welfare state. All that is needed is a change of mind-set, so that it can become accepted that basic income is a form of universal security like public education and health. Basic income is a design change – a small change to our institutions. But it is an important change, in terms of recognising humanity as the basis on which societies function or fall apart.

Basic income and the democratisation of development in Europe

26, part I

The Indian experience: the debt trap and unconditional basic income

Sarath Davala, India

'Basic income has a strong positive effect on households caught in perennial debt. It is not that basic income helps the households to pay off their debt altogether. The effect is incremental. Being paid monthly creates a sense of income security for basic day-to-day needs. This psychological effect gradually enables people to make strategic choices about their employment and sources of borrowing, that eventually have far-reaching effects.'

The MP-UBI Pilot Study, carried out between 2011 and 2013, funded by UNICEF and coordinated by the Self-Employed Women's Association (SEWA) - a national federation of women workers' trade unions in the informal sector with a membership of nearly two million - comprised two parallel pilots. The first, larger pilot, was conducted in eight general caste villages. The second in a Bhil tribal village. In these nine villages, all individuals were paid a modest unconditional basic income each month, with the payment for children under 18 paid to the mother or a designated guardian. 'Control' villages with similar socio-economic characteristics were selected where basic income was not paid.

In the first pilot, during the first 12 months Rs. 200 (roughly £2.40) was paid to every adult and half of that amount to children under 18. For the next five months, the amount was increased to Rs. 300 (roughly £3.60). In the tribal pilot, for a period of 12 months, Rs. 300 was paid to each adult and half of that amount to children. In both the pilots together, about 6,000 individuals from about 1,100 households received a monthly basic income.

A baseline survey census, an interim and a final evaluation survey were conducted to evaluate the situation of the recipients, before, during and after the basic income transfers. These surveys were also conducted in the 'control' villages. In total, the surveys covered over 15,000 individuals. In addition, 100 in-depth case studies were carried out during the experiment as were interviews with key respondents. The pilots had five main features:

1. The basic income transfers were to individuals.
2. The transfers were universal – everyone in the selected village received the basic income.
3. The transfers were unconditional.
4. Money in the first pilot was paid in to a bank account which in most cases, particularly for women, was opened especially for the project; in the case of the tribal village, money was paid directly to people in cash since the bank was far away from the village.
5. The transfers were on a monthly basis.

In the first pilot, money was paid from June 2011 to November 2012; in the tribal village, money was paid from February 2012 to January 2013.

Debt trap

In the pilot villages, most households have been caught in a debt trap, and find it extremely difficult to get out of it. Typically, it happens like this. A health shock, or any major life event in the family – from a birth to a wedding or a death – is usually the starting point. To pay for such events, money is borrowed from landlords in their own or neighbouring village. If they have land, they mortgage the land, and most cases where there are no assets, they borrow on the basis of their promise of future labour. In other words, they mortgage their bodies. The moneylender charges a monthly interest rate of 2–10%.

The borrowers begin to work for the landlord (usually on a farm or in a brick-kiln). Since the individual or family labour is provided to the landlord as a repayment of a loan, there are technically no wages paid. To survive, the family again borrows small amounts for everyday expenses, often buying from a landlord's grocery store on credit. So, these small borrowings continue. The accounts are settled annually, at which point the worker finds out whether the landlord owes him any wage or he still has some more balance of the original loan to repay.

That is how the vicious debt cycle perpetuates. Very few people ever escape this quagmire of debt. The local term for people who are in such debt bondage is *Naukar*, which literally means 'a servant', but also has the connotations of 'a slave'.

Unconditional basic income

One of the major aspects tested in the pilot was the effect of an unconditional basic income on this debt bondage. The main findings were:[35]

- At the outset, three-quarters of the recipient households reported being in some form of financial debt.
- As the pilot progressed the households receiving basic income were less likely to have increased their debt and were more likely to have reduced it since they immediately stop the small borrowings for everyday needs.
- Basic income households try to move away from the exploitative sources of borrowing to softer sources such as friends and relatives, since the basic income transfers makes them credit-worthy in the community.

This early impact prepares the ground for several other effects. First, a sense of income security develops with less worry about daily provisions. Second, this state of mind leads to better planning, enabling cultivation of their land without borrowing. So, they save for the seeds. Although Rs. 300 per head per month may not seem like much money, a family of six with four adults and two children gets about Rs. 1500. If a household pool and save the money for 3 months before the sowing season, they have enough for the seeds and also other incidental costs.

The story of the small farmers of Ghodakhurd – the tribal pilot village – illustrates this pattern. The typical land-holding in Ghodakhurd is 2 to 5 bighas, between half an acre and one acre.[36] Almost every household owns some land, except for a few who have mortgaged it, and perhaps lost it in the process. For seeds and fertilisers, Ghodakhurd farmers used to be mostly dependent on a particular local landlord-cum-moneylender. The entire village used to be at his door to borrow for seed and later, for fertiliser. The year villagers got basic income, they completely snapped their dependence on the landlord-cum-moneylender.

When this author recently (April 2017) visited the village for a follow-up study, the farmers reported that only 5 or 6 farmers – out of about 100 – in the entire village still went to the moneylender for seeds and fertilisers. This shift has been dramatic and continues even after four years. Small farmers have snapped at least one type of dependence.

While the above is a village level phenomenon, there are also behavioural shifts in several individual households. Here is another illustration from Hariram, a typical debt-ridden agricultural worker from Ghodakhurd village. Hariram and his wife Manjubai are landless labourers. Some years ago, Manjubai developed an illness in her joints which prevented her from taking up any paid work. Hariram became the sole earner in the family. Hariram has been a *Naukar* with a big farmer for a while. He said:

'The employment options within the village are limited, so we have to look for wage work in neighbouring villages. Nobody likes to work as a Naukar, but my situation is

The Indian experience: the debt trap and unconditional basic income particularly bad because of not having land of my own and my wife's illness. Last year she had a hip replacement. Now the other hip needs replacing. We have been in debt continuously. As soon as the basic income started, we could pay for everyday needs, so I went to the brick-kiln because there I get at least 200 rupees a day; and more importantly if there is a medical emergency, I can borrow from the brick-kiln owner.

After working in the brick-kiln that year, I realised that life was too hard there, and since my family was managing their daily food requirements using the basic income, I asked myself why I should continue as a bonded labourer. Normally, the facility of borrowing easily is what makes that job attractive. Since the basic needs were met, I looked for better work and ended up working for a shop-keeper about 4 kilometres from my village. He also has a farm, so I sometimes work on that. He is a nice man, and he also lets me borrow from him without interest. Today, I am not a bonded labourer. Basic income made us less desperate, and made me think that it is possible to choose another kind of work. Even now, I have debts, but the quality of my employment has changed.'

Basic income has a strong positive effect on households caught in perennial debt. It is not that basic income helps the households to pay off their debt altogether. The effect is incremental. Being paid monthly creates a sense of income security for basic day-to-day needs. This psychological effect gradually enables people to make strategic choices about their employment and sources of borrowing, that eventually have far-reaching effects. The experiment was for a short duration of 12–17 months. However, if we project the trend, it is probable that, at least in some households, one could imagine more sustained effects. Further, by being unconditional, the cash has enabled households to make their own rational choices that improve their overall situation. This is why unconditional basic income has great potential to address poverty.

The Indian experience: the debt trap and unconditional basic income

26, part II

The Indian experience:
the impact of universal basic income
on women and girls

Soumya Kapoor Mehta, India

'One of the most important findings was the emancipatory effect basic income had on groups such as women and children who otherwise have limited voice in decision-making both within the household, and in the community.'

The idea of universal basic income (UBI) is currently creating a lot of buzz in Indian policy circles. While the incumbent government has been vociferous in claiming that the idea has some merit, others have criticised it as likely to have very adverse fiscal implications. There have also been debates on whether UBI is a more effective way of reaching India's poor than the current complex plethora of subsidies that rest on conditionalities and have been criticised for sluggish delivery. Those who oppose the idea feel it is only an excuse to truncate the welfare state. Irrespective of whether the views come from the left or right, many others believe that UBI's time has come.

Any proposal to implement an Indian scheme can learn from the lessons of the Madhya Pradesh pilot. The experiment paid all individuals - rich, poor, elderly, women, children, differently abled, those belonging to vulnerable caste groups – the same amount. Crucially, there were no conditions on how the monthly payments 'should' be spent. The targeted recipients were informed in advance that they could use the money as they wished, and that there would be no direction from the pilot team. The money was transferred directly either into a bank or a SEWA cooperative account.

Conditions were done away with for two reasons. First, research on conditional cash transfers shows that conditionalities are often expensive to implement. Secondly, the research team wanted to test the hypothesis that people are generally capable of making their own decisions and do so in the best interests of themselves and their families, rather than spending it on 'private bads' such as alcohol. That this hypothesis held true was one of the strongest findings of the study, and has resonated with top policymakers in India.

The evaluation drew primarily on panel survey data, case studies, community level surveys and interviews, but also included the tracking of children's weight-for-age (as a proxy for nutrition) and their attendance and performance in schools.[37]

One of the most important findings was the emancipatory effect basic income had on groups such as women and children who otherwise have limited voice in decision-making both within the household, and in the community. The pilot involved three features rarely found in social policy, which taken together provided women, in particular, with increased choices. First, the payment was to individuals and so the woman had greater control over the money, or at the very minimum an influence on how it was spent. Second, the amount was equal for men and women, which made the experiment progressive in gender terms, since the average income of women in India is lower than that of men. If they were mothers, the women received the basic income of the children as well, giving greater control, potentially, over spending decisions for their children. Third, as the basic income was unconditional, in principle women as well as men had a choice on how to spend the money.

One of the first empowering effects was visible at the start of the pilot. Some households refused to take the basic income. They were mainly rich farmers who said they did not need the money, did not want to open individual bank accounts for their women, or that taking 'free money' was against their religion and below their dignity. However, upon learning the refusal of their men folk, the women within these households came forward and said they wanted the cash transfer.

It seemed the women put the extra cash to good use. The pilot found encouraging evidence on reduction in children's malnutrition levels. Nutrition for girls and women in India has been considered less important than for boys and men. Receipt of basic income, however, had a statistically significant impact on children's nutrition, particularly for girls. Before the basic income transfers started, the proportion of normal weight-for-age children in the recipient villages under the general pilot was lower than in control villages (39% compared to 48%). However, by the end of the intervention, the proportion in the former set of villages had risen by 19 percentage points (from 39% to 58%). In comparison, the increase in control villages was a modest 10 percentage points (from 48% to 58%). Further, while the nutritional status of boys improved in both types of villages, there was a significant rise in the proportion of girls with normal weight-for-age in basic income villages (a 25 percentage point improvement compared to 12 percentage point improvement in control villages).

The case studies revealed that the basic income had improved a household's capacity to buy from the market, resulting in a qualitative shift in their food basket with, for example, more spent on fresh vegetables and milk.

The basic income payment also had a salutary impact on school enrolment levels, particularly that of girls. One of the strongest findings was the fall in the number of households pulling girls out of schools. While only 36% of girls of secondary school going age were enrolled in schools in the control villages in the general pilot, nearly 66% of girls of the same age cohort were going to school in basic income villages by the end of the intervention.

Receipt of basic income also facilitated an increase in school spending – on items such as uniforms, shoes, and books in both the general and tribal pilots. The case studies provided testimony on how small expenditures, such as those on shoes, helped children overcome barriers (specifically poor appearance) to attendance. No longer 'dirty' or unkempt, children from poor households could now attend schools without a sense of 'shame'. Along with an increase in schooling, the basic income also led to a reduction in child labour in the villages receiving the transfer. Finally, women who received the basic income increased their labour and work relative to women who did not receive such a transfer.

To conclude, the Madhya Pradesh pilots revealed that basic income benefits can be substantial and build on one another. For example, women with more cash can buy seeds and take up farming while children in school need not engage in child labour and are better nourished. However, basic income is not a panacea for 'failing' social policies. Introduction of basic income also does not mean lowering of state benefits or rolling back state commitment to improving the welfare of its population. Basic income must be seen as progressive, and not as a step towards dismantling public and universal social services. It will be interesting to see how the Indian government takes up the idea.

27

A Scottish pilot

Annie Miller, Scotland

'Reports in the media often give the impression that the Scottish Basic Income Project is a done deal, and about to happen immediately – as if by magic. This belies the fact that very important preparatory work has still to be carried out during the planning phase. It is crucial to its success that this preparatory work is well thought through and thorough.'

Interest in basic income (BI) has been increasing steadily in Scotland in recent years. The Scottish Green Party presented a costed BI scheme in August 2014. A Scottish think-tank, Reform Scotland, produced a scheme for Scotland.[38] Although the Scottish National Party (SNP) passed a resolution in favour of BI at its 2016 conference, the SNP government has not yet adopted it as policy. The Scottish Greens included a scheme in its 2017 general election manifesto.

In November 2015, Fife Council published a report on poverty entitled *Fairer Fife*,[39] which included a brief statement of its willingness to host a pilot. In May 2016, the economist Guy Standing, who had played an important role in the Namibia and Indian pilots, was invited to give the Angus Millar Lecture in Edinburgh, hosted by the Royal Society for the Encouragement of Arts, Manufactures and Commerce (RSA) in Scotland.

In the meantime, the Citizen's Basic Income Network Scotland (CBINS), formed in late 2015, held a launch meeting in Govan, Glasgow, on 26 November 2016. During a panel session, Glasgow Councillor Matt Kerr's announcement that Glasgow Council would also host a BI experiment was greeted with great excitement. Matt has gathered together a cross-party group of councillors to progress this plan. The meeting was such a success that CBINS organised a second launch in conjunction with Fife Council in January 2017, attended by many local people.

Both Fife and the City of Glasgow Councils have cross-party support for a BI experiment, and both have delegated responsibility to council officials to progress it further, avoiding any potentially-conflicting party political influences. Each has been supported by a think-tank. City of Glasgow is supported by RSA in Scotland, which is supportive of a BI. Jamie Cooke, head of RSA in Scotland, and Sandra McDermott, Director of Financial Inclusion for Glasgow Council, have initiated several meetings on BI in Glasgow for third sector organisations and ordinary citizens, including benefit recipients.

Similarly, Paul Vaughan, Head of Communities and Neighbourhoods in Fife, is responsible for progressing the idea, and has organised meetings for councillors, local businesses and residents. Fife Council has circulated a questionnaire to a sample of local people that serves both to gauge current attitudes and to educate the population. Fife Council is supported by the Fife-based Carnegie Foundation, founded by the wealthy industrialist and philanthropist, Andrew Carnegie. Earlier in 2017, North Ayrshire announced its wish to host a BI experiment, but has not yet had the same opportunity to connect with its population. There is also the possibility that the City of Edinburgh might wish to throw its hat in the ring. This would mean that the three largest councils in Scotland (Glasgow, Edinburgh and Fife) could be involved in a Scottish experiment.

A BI is defined as being based on the individual, universal, not means-tested, non-selective and unconditional. However, this definition merely defines a class of income maintenance systems, and further prioritised objectives, assumptions and constraints are necessary to design an actual scheme, including how it is to be financed. An authentic BI experiment would cover all age groups and all income groups, and include the intended method of financing it. In order to gauge the effects on sample subjects, the experiment should test different levels of BI, especially for working-age people, and the corresponding levels of the intended method of funding. It should also be such that it could be rolled out at a national level.

Reports in the media often give the impression that the Scottish Basic Income Project is a done deal, and about to happen immediately – as if by magic. This belies the fact that very important preparatory work has still to be carried out during the planning phase. It is crucial to its success that this preparatory work is well thought through and thorough, and should not be rushed.

During this planning phase, four processes must take place in parallel:

- Planning the actual BI schemes that would be implemented and the results of which would later be analysed.
- A public education programme to ensure support for the project by an informed population.
- A political process must be undergone, to ensure that first the councils, and then the Scottish Government and other official bodies, will back the plan devised by the planning team.
- An eye must be kept open for potential financial resources.

The process of planning the project needs to be detailed, and seed-corn money will be required for this. A research team (comprising a statistician specialising in experimental design, an economist, a psychologist, a social security expert, among others) would work closely together throughout the project. The team would build on the groundwork of the participating councils and their support groups.

The team's brief should be to list the outcomes that the participating councils want a BI scheme to achieve; design one (or more) BI scheme that could fulfil these desired objectives; list the

A Scottish pilot

147

questions to which answers are required; translate the questions into hypotheses to test; design and test a questionnaire that can be put to the sample subjects at regular intervals throughout the experiment; ensure that the results collected through interviews and questionnaires are such that the hypotheses can be tested.

The project should be a unified one with variations among the councils to test different aspects of the scheme, while avoiding unnecessary repetition. The team would also be able to draw on the experience and evidence from the other country pilots being undertaken.

The team would also work out the interventions required (such as a baseline survey of the whole community to collect data about its characteristics; public information meetings to get the community involved and committed; the frequency with which sample subjects would be interviewed or presented with a questionnaire; and case studies).They would advise on the duration of the project, sample sizes and control groups, in order to be able to answer all the questions, and to ensure that the analysis would be statistically rigorous.

The team would also be asked to estimate a realistic cost of the project. This should include administration costs for the implementation of the scheme and the various support workers. The sample sizes, the generosity of the BI schemes and duration of the project will determine the sum of gross transfer payments (i.e. the overall cost) of the actual BI schemes. But the cost of the project will also include the cost of the research team and their field workers for the duration of the experiment and for a couple of years afterwards to collate and analyse the data and disseminate the results. Potential sources of financing the project will also have to be explored.

An educational programme must address all sectors of society, including politicians and policymakers, civil servants and council officials, opinion-formers, media, voluntary sector organisations, churches, trades unions, and the general public, including many who rely on benefits. It would define a BI and describe the broad objectives to which it could contribute, give justifications for a BI scheme, the criticisms often levelled at BI, and their counter-arguments. CBINS has a programme for training people who would like to become BI advocates and learn enough about the subject to field difficult questions and put forward the facts with conviction. Rather than forming specific BI groups around the country, CBINS would prefer advocates and other knowledgeable persons to discuss BI with others within their own spheres of interest and influence.

The political process is based on enough constituents who are keen on BI being prepared to build up relationships with their local councillors, Members of the Scottish Parliament and of the Westminster Parliament – in effect educating their elected representatives about BI.

It is only after all of these processes have taken place, probably taking between two and three years, that the planning team can return to the officials of the participating councils, who would then ask the well-briefed councillors to sign off the proposal. Similarly, when the time comes for the councils to approach the Scottish Government to underwrite the Scottish BI Project, and to ask the Westminster Government, Her Majesty's Treasury, Her Majesty's Revenue and Customs and the Department for Work and Pensions to accommodate the experiment, the relevant politicians will also be well-primed.

There is a long way to go, and many hurdles to clear, before a Scottish pilot can go ahead. Determination and persistence are necessary from those who are keen for a *bona fide* experiment to take place in Scotland in order to sustain all those involved through the process.

A Scottish pilot

28

The libertarian case for universal basic income

Matt Zwolinski, USA

'... there's a good case to be made for having two distinct basic income type policies. One would be a small, truly universal cash grant ... The other would be a less universal but more generous grant directed toward those individuals who fall below a certain specified threshold of economic sufficiency.'

Libertarianism is a political philosophy which holds the protection of individual liberty to be the highest political end. Because of this commitment, and because they regard the coercive power of government as one of the most serious threats to individual liberty, libertarians generally believe that the legitimate powers of the government are quite strictly limited. For some libertarians, this means that the most extensive justifiable state is a 'minimal' state devoted to the protection of individuals against force and fraud. Such a state will support a police force, a military, and a court system in order to protect its citizens' rights of person and property. But that is all. Other libertarians (perhaps better referred to as 'classical liberals') believe in a somewhat more expansive role for the state – adding the provision of public goods and perhaps a basic form of social safety net to the list of permissible state activities. And still others (known sometimes as anarcho-capitalists or market anarchists) believe that the only permissible state is no state at all, and that whatever protective services individuals wish to consume must be purchased or otherwise obtained by voluntary, non-coercive means.

For the most part, libertarians are strongly opposed to any form of state-based welfare. For some, opposition to state-financed welfare is a matter of fundamental moral principle. 'Taxation is theft', they say, and so any redistributive measures that involve taxation are themselves a kind of theft, and therefore a violation of individual rights.[40] Others base their opposition to the welfare state on more pragmatic considerations, holding that the problem with welfare is the *effects* it produces on taxpayers, recipients, and society as a whole. But whatever the source of their opposition, opposition to the welfare state is an essential tenet of libertarianism.

I think that view is a mistake,[41] both historically and philosophically. As a matter of intellectual history, there are a number of important libertarian thinkers who have supported some form of welfare state. Milton Friedman, Friedrich Hayek, and even the much-maligned Herbert Spencer all favoured some form of state relief to the poor – the former two even advocating something that looks a lot like a basic income guarantee. And as a matter of good normative philosophy, I think they were probably on to something!

I think there are two strong libertarian arguments in support of a basic income, one broadly deontological in nature and the other broadly consequentialist. The deontological argument has to do with the limits to the libertarian case for private property. For reasons that I think were very well laid out by Herbert Spencer in 1851,[42] I don't think the standard Lockean story about self-ownership and labour mixing gets us very far in justifying private property in land and other natural resources. For starters, that account simply doesn't match the historical reality in which most private property originated in force and theft rather than peaceful homesteading. But, more fundamentally, I just don't see how mixing your labour in a natural object gets you a property right in the whole economic value of that object, as opposed to a right to that portion of the value created by your labour. Basically, I think the radical American 19th century economist Henry George – who argued for a 'land value tax' to capture the unearned increased in land values for wider public benefit – was right.[43] And so I think that there's a strong case to be made for a basic income funded by a 'Single Tax' on 'land rent' – the economic value of unimproved natural resources such as land.

The more consequentialist case has to do with protecting individual freedom. I call it a consequentialist case rather than a utilitarian one deliberately. The idea is that a basic income can help protect the freedom of certain vulnerable people. But I recognise that a basic income that's large and broad enough to do that might have to be funded by taxes that violate the freedom of others. So we're trading off freedom for freedom. That might sound scary to some libertarians, but I think that unless you're an anarchist you're already willing to accept something like this. Tax-funded police services, after all, protect individual freedom but are funded by coercive taxation.

I think the seeds for a freedom-based defence of a basic income are present in the writings of Friedrich Hayek, especially in his Constitution of Liberty.[44] Hayek himself defended a kind of basic income, but was never entirely clear about what he saw the justification for it to be. I've tried to work out what a plausible Hayekian justification might be, at least in terms of broad outlines.[45] I see Hayek as embracing a kind of republican account of liberty, where freedom means not just not being subject to the initiation of force but, more generally, not being subject to the arbitrary will of any other person. Once you take that account of freedom on board, I think you can justify a basic income as a way of protecting the economically vulnerable. The idea is that people who might otherwise have to accept any offer an employer makes or else starve aren't really free. A basic income gives them the ability to say 'no,' and thus protects them from being bossed around by the economically powerful.

One interesting thing to note about these two arguments is that they're not just different in terms of where they start – the moral premises on which they're based. I think they're also different in terms of where they end up – in the kind of basic income they justify. If the Georgist argument works, I think that justifies a truly universal basic income. The earth belongs to all of us, and so all of us have an equal claim to the economic value of unimproved natural resources. Now, depending on how much of present wealth you think is due to labour, rather than raw natural resources, the value of this kind of basic income might not be very large. So, on this argument, what you might end up with is a very broad but relatively small basic income. Everybody gets something, but nobody gets much.

The freedom-based argument, on the other hand, doesn't give us any reason to write a cheque to Bill Gates. His freedom is already protected by his economic power, so there's no real point in giving him any more money. And the same will be true of a lot of other people, not just the rich but probably most of the middle class as well. So if the case for a basic income is based on the protection of individual freedom, I think what that gets you is something less than a universal basic income. Not everybody gets something, but what those who need it get will be large enough to effectively protect them against economic domination by others.

Now, given these two distinct moral considerations that justify a basic income, I think that there's a good case to be made for having two distinct basic income type policies that respond to those considerations. One would be a small, truly universal cash grant based on the economic value of unimproved natural resources. Think of this as something like the Alaskan Permanent Fund writ large. The other would be a less universal but more generous grant directed toward those individuals who fall below a certain specified threshold of economic sufficiency. I think the best way of implementing this second programme is probably something like Milton Friedman's Negative Income Tax,[46] though I also like the proposal set forth by Charles Murray in his book, *In Our Hands*.[47]

In both cases, people earning less than a certain amount of money get a cash grant from the government, with which they can do whatever they wish; while people earning more than that amount get nothing. That conditionality makes the programme less than truly universal. But I think you've got to do something like that in order to make a basic income economically feasible. Many basic income enthusiasts want a grant that is (1) universal, (2) large enough to provide people with an adequate level of income, and (3) economically affordable. But you can't satisfy all three of those conditions at once. A Negative Income Tax satisfies conditions (2) and (3), which to my mind are the most important conditions, morally speaking. Condition (1) might be politically important in terms of generating and sustaining support for the programme. I'm not sure. But it seems to me that something has to give, and I think there's a strong case to be made for keeping (2) and (3) and relegating (1) to the land-tax component of the joint programme.

29

For us all: redesigning social security for the 2020s

Andrew Harrop, Fabian Society, UK

'In the UK a UBI becomes an affordable proposition when it is thought of not as a vast new spending programme, but as a process for integrating and rationalising existing entitlements that are already of broadly similar generosity.'

The debate on universal basic income (UBI) may be global, but concrete proposals for reform must be tied to local circumstances. In the UK, the conditions are right for the introduction of a modest basic income instead of tax allowances, set below a subsistence level. But introducing a full UBI, to replace most means-tested benefits, would either be unaffordable or would bring no extra help to low income households.

When you look at the UK's tax and benefit systems together, the country has a broadly flat-rate regime for supporting household living standards which helps rich and poor alike. People with low incomes mainly receive means-tested benefits, while middle- to high-income households mainly receive tax-free allowances. But the total level of support is much the same. For example, by 2020, the tax allowances that exempt the first portion of earnings from tax will be worth £68 per week, compared to £73 per week for the basic out-of-work benefit.

So should politicians seek to merge the two systems to create a single flat-rate payment: a British version of universal basic income? The idea of a UBI is that every adult and child should receive a single flat-rate subsistence payment from the government, in place of both tax-free allowances and means-tested benefits. The payment would then be gradually offset by taxation, using a single marginal rate of withdrawal. In the UK a UBI becomes an affordable proposition when it is thought of not as a vast new spending programme, but as a process for integrating and rationalising existing entitlements that are already of broadly similar generosity. The task would be to combine the main tax allowances and benefits in a way that was broadly revenue neutral, since significant increases in tax rates would be unlikely to attract public support (and even if they did, extra spending on public services would be a higher priority).

The case is unproven for a fully-fledged UBI, which replaces most means-tested benefits *and* tax allowances. This is because a basic income along these lines would not be an egalitarian, poverty-reducing policy. Its introduction would be a huge administrative reform but would leave the overall income distribution and the incidence of poverty no better than it is today. Indeed, modelling for the Compass pressure group (see Chapter 30) found that a full basic income would result in many 'losers' among low income groups and a rise in child poverty.[48] Those in the deepest poverty – people out of work for long periods of time – would not see their incomes rise, because a full basic income would simply replace Universal Credit. And if increments for incapacity and other special circumstances ended, some people without work might even end up worse off. Meanwhile, many households with low or middle earnings would also lose in cases where the value of their UBI was outweighed by their extra tax liabilities and reduced in-work benefits. And in the UK, we could not expect behavioural responses to a UBI to improve matters much, since the country already has record levels of employment and a rising minimum wage.

Nor could a British basic income ever live up to the ambition to end the need for means-tested benefits. In the UK, housing costs are both very high and very variable. This means that it would be implausibly expensive to provide everyone with a basic income sufficient to cover a cheap rent in the typical housing market. And even if this did happen, anyone in more expensive areas would still be unable to meet their housing costs. So a complete end to means testing is a non-starter. This may be a cause of frustration for supporters of UBI in all its theoretical purity. But it is also an opportunity for real-world reformers, because it forces us to stop thinking about basic income and means testing as an 'either/or' choice. If means testing in the UK is inevitable, then a basic income has to be seen as just one element in a broader system of social security. The question becomes what should be the balance between universal, means-tested (and also contributory) forms of support.

This is the thinking behind recent proposals from the Fabian Society, which suggested that a modest universal payment should be paid to everyone, alongside continued means-tested payments for low income households.[49] Our plan is to retain means-tested Universal Credit and create a basic income using the revenue from tax allowances and child benefit alone. The money would be sufficient to fund a substantial minimum payment.

For example, if the reform was introduced overnight in 2020, it might be possible to pay every working-age adult *and* child around £40 per week, in place of the £68 of tax allowance that just goes to those with sufficient earnings. Since tax allowances are much more regressive than universal payments, this would be a significant redistribution from rich to poor. But, importantly, it would also redistribute resources from men to women, and from households without children to those with them. It would involve a substantial increase in the current level of child benefit, itself an important step in reducing the level of child poverty. If this system was introduced with the credits for adults and children each set at around £40 per week, a two-parent family of four would have a stable baseline income of £160, before net earnings or means-tested additions.

By substituting a basic income for regressive tax allowances, while leaving progressive benefits in place, the Fabian strategy would substantially raise the living standards of low income households. Today we have a system where a single pensioner receives twice as much as a single person seeking work. The first priority for egalitarians must be to 'level-up', so that we offer real subsistence incomes for all. In the British context, swapping Universal Credit with a basic income would be a huge distraction from this task. Instead, the Fabian plan creates a tiered system, where the universal and mean-tested payments would combine together to provide a humane minimum income.

This package would substantially reduce child poverty and income inequality. But in practice it could not be introduced overnight, because it would create a large number of cash 'losers', including many with quite low incomes. Our proposal is therefore that the basic income should be introduced gradually over, perhaps, 15 years. The tax-free allowances would be progressively reduced in value and each year there would be a matching increase in the basic income, leaving no one worse off in cash terms. The goal would be to devote the same share of national economic output to the basic income as we currently give to the tax-free allowances and child benefit (around 5% of GDP). The rate of economic growth and inflation would dictate how long the transition would take – the higher each is, the faster the pace of change, while avoiding cash losers. To start with, people would be paid just a few pounds per week, but eventually the basic income would rise towards the original cash value of the tax-free allowances.

This is a basic income proposal for reformers focused on ends not means. It is a gradualist strategy for transferring huge resources between income groups and massively reducing poverty, without anyone being left out of pocket in cash terms. Yes, it sacrifices the theoretical purity of a fully-fledged UBI. But for the prize of higher living standards in Britain, that is a price worth paying.

30

Making universal basic income work: the incremental approach

Stewart Lansley and Howard Reed, UK

'"Starting small" through an incremental approach has many benefits. Such an approach is grounded in reality. By building on the existing system, it offers an incremental, phased approach to reform, ... [and] reduces the risks of reform, while offering flexibility for gradual improvements over time.'

Now that there is growing momentum behind the idea of a UBI, the debate is turning to implementation and to the practical questions of how to make UBI a reality. Two of the big issues are whether it is affordable and whether it could deliver a more progressive system of social protection that reduces poverty.

Some critics say it would fail these two tests: as Emran Mian in the *Independent* has put it, 'the utopia it promises is a deceit'. An affordable UBI, it is claimed, would not pay enough to be worth the bother of change, while one which paid a decent rate would be much too expensive.[50] To find out if 'deceit' is at work, we have modelled two different approaches to implementation for the progressive pressure group Compass.[51] The first tested a 'full UBI scheme', one which replaces most, though not all, benefits including most means-tested benefits.[52] The second tested a 'modified scheme', one which leaves most of the existing system, including means-tested benefits, in place. This second approach can be seen as a first step towards the gradual implementation of a fuller scheme.

Both approaches have been evaluated according to the net cost, the number and pattern of gainers and losers and the impact on poverty and on inequality. These simulations show that a full and generous scheme, one that swept away most of the existing system of income support in one go – a 'big bang' approach – would be either too expensive, or create too many losers among lower income households, thus raising poverty levels. This is because the current benefits system, partly due to its reliance on means testing, is able to deliver large sums to some groups. These problems suggest that a full scheme structured in these ways is not feasible in the current circumstances.

An incremental approach

However, the study also found that a 'modified' scheme, one that still provided a universal and unconditional income, albeit at a moderate starting level, and that initially left much of the existing system intact, would be feasible. Payments were set at £51 per week for pensioners, £71 for adults over 25 and £61 for those under 25, and £59 for children. This approach would keep nearly all existing benefits while UBI is taken into account as income when calculating means-tested benefits. It would reduce dependence on means testing by taking into account the citizen's payment when calculating benefits.

Such a scheme – while not a silver bullet – would offer real and substantial gains:

- a sharp increase in average income among the poorest
- a cut in child poverty of 45%
- a modest reduction in inequality
- a strengthening of the universal element of the benefit system with a fall of a fifth in the number of families claiming means-tested benefits.

The impact of the modified scheme is the product of two key changes: the replacement of the personal tax allowance (of no benefit to those with earnings below the tax threshold) with a flat-rate payment to all, and changes in tax and national insurance contributions (NICs). Marginal income tax rates are increased, with the basic and higher rates rising from their current 20% and 40% to 25% and 45% respectively. The national insurance lower earnings limit is abolished and the rate of employee NICs increased to 12% across the whole earnings scale, effectively abolishing the upper earnings limit. In addition, conditional benefits are made unconditional.

These changes produce a more progressive and integrated tax-benefit system, with reductions in poverty and inequality, a strengthening of universalism, and more of the role of means testing shifted to the tax system.

The modified scheme has a net cost of around £8bn per year, just under 0.5% of GDP. This is a modest sum in the context of overall public spending and the significant reduction in poverty and inequality it delivers, while reaping many – if not all – the benefits of a full UBI. It would reduce the level of child poverty on one widely used measure (those in households falling below 60% of median net household income, before housing costs) to below a tenth, less than the level for any year since 1961.[53]

The cost is well within the range of normal fiscal adjustment and compared with the potential revenue from other tax changes.[54] It is also modest when compared with the cost of other recent tax changes. Government tax cuts during 2015/16 (a period of fiscal austerity) – an increase in the personal allowance, a cut in the corporation tax rate and cuts in fuel duties – cost an additional £19.5bn.[55]

The results are based on a static analysis, assuming no behavioural effects in response to the introduction of UBI and the tax changes. In practice, there would be dynamic behavioural effects, including on employment. Such a scheme would be a hybrid. Although it would retain some of the complexity of the existing system, it would contain a genuine unconditional

Making universal basic income work: the incremental approach income and would deliver many of the benefits of an ideal scheme.

Incrementalism

Some critics of UBI have a point. It would be difficult to implement a full-blooded, big bang scheme. But there is more than one route to implementation. 'Starting small' through an incremental approach has many benefits. Such an approach is grounded in reality. By building on the existing system, it offers an incremental, phased approach to reform, not wholescale and immediate replacement. Some proponents of change have described this approach as too cautious, as 'dreaming small'. But incrementalism reduces the risks of reform, while offering flexibility for gradual improvements over time. It could, for example, be phased in by starting with modest payments that are gradually improved over time. Alternatively it could be phased by demographic group, perhaps starting with a stand-alone scheme for children through a big increase in the level of child benefit. This is evolution, not revolution.

Child benefit is effectively a basic income for children, and there is a strong case for raising the level of child benefit substantially (it is set to have lost a quarter of its real value between 2010 and 2020) as a particularly effective way of reducing poverty, as well as being a first step of a UBI. Most left opponents of a UBI would accept the progressive merits of raising child benefit.

There are further advantages of a process of gradual implementation. We have learnt from previous social experiments that large scale, big bang changes – such as the introduction of Universal Credit – can have quite significant negative immediate effects on families along with unintended consequences. Under a gradual approach, later phases could learn the lessons of the impact of the first phase and appropriate adjustments made.

In this way, the actual execution of a scheme over time would be accompanied, in effect, by a real, full-scale trial in which the impact is monitored on an ongoing basis, before moving to a fuller model. This approach would enable an ongoing evaluation of a range of aspects of implementation: on poverty, inequality and the level of means testing; on the effectiveness of the administration; and, crucially, on some of the widely debated issues, including the impact on work incentives, on lifestyle choices and on the bargaining power of labour. This would also enable an evaluation of the kind of choices being made – between work, education, training, caring, leisure and voluntary work at different stages of implementation.

PART V:
THE YEAR OF
THE TRIALS

31

An earthquake in Finland

Otto Lehto, Finland

'The political legacy of the Finnish experiment, as a symbolic herald of future reforms, may outlive its narrow scientific usefulness.'

The Finnish experiment of 2017-18 is a crucial test case. It provides one of the most robust experimental tests of a universal basic income (UBI) in the context of an advanced industrialised society. And it *is* a real milestone, since it represents a non-utopian approach to UBI that can be palatable to middle class voters. But its partial success is also a partial failure. Although it is too early to render judgement, the Finnish case shows that there are many obstacles for the successful implementation of theoretical models. Experiments often fall short of the ideal experimental conditions. This speaks against taking too optimistic a view on the next step.

There is a widespread consensus in Finland that the welfare state, and its benefit structure, should be organised according to 'labourist' principles. In practice, this means that working age people who are not incapacitated by a medical condition should be heavily incentivised to work - whether directly compelled or indirectly nudged - in exchange for being eligible for benefits. This explains why the Finnish experiment has been framed, almost exclusively, in terms of work incentives. However, it is good to keep in mind that the UBI model used in the experiment, *if* given to all citizens, would be an improvement over the current Finnish benefit system, since it comes surprisingly close to satisfying the orthodox conditions of a UBI scheme: it is given automatically and without means testing; it provides a predictable long-term safety net; and it is not withheld or deducted from people who take up part-time or full-time work.[1]

How to generate an earthquake

There has been a long sequence of public debate on UBI in Finland since the 1980s. The idea has been a surprisingly persistent thorn in the side of the establishment. In fact, the only reason that the government is experimenting is because of long-term pressure from civil society. The legitimacy of UBI had been slowly established through bursts of support from all sides of the ideological spectrum. Discussed over many years, the vast majority of the population had heard of UBI and it does not seem utopian to them. In fact, popular support for UBI in Finland has been apparent for a long time.

In 2013, BIEN Finland collected 22,000 signatures for a UBI citizen's initiative that created a media buzz, although it failed to reach the required threshold to be taken up by Parliament. In addition to public pressure, much of the credit goes to opposition parties. In 2014, the Green Party presented a UBI proposal set at €560 a month – not coincidentally the exact same figure as the one eventually chosen for the experiment. Other groups, including the Left Alliance and the think-tank Libera, have also produced their own UBI models. In 2014, the idea for a UBI experiment was pushed conspicuously by the think-tanks Tänk and Sitra.[2]

In the 2015 parliamentary elections, the agrarian and centrist Centre Party (Keskusta) emerged victorious and Juha Sipilä became the new prime minister. Sipilä's cautious pro-UBI stance reawakened the largely dormant and silent support for UBI that has existed within the Centre Party for decades. Sipilä forged a government coalition with the centre-right National

Coalition Party (Kokoomus) and the right-wing nationalist and populist party – The Finns Party – formerly known as True Finns (Perussuomalaiset). Sipilä's coalition partners have been more sceptical of UBI, but not officially against it.

The Finnish experiment, running from January 2017 to December 2018, through the government's semi-independent welfare bureaucratic organ, KELA (The Social Insurance Institution of Finland), consists of giving an unconditional basic income grant of €560 a month to 2,000 randomly selected individuals between the ages of 25 and 58, across the country. Those selected were official recipients of the government's unemployment benefits during the time of the selection process. Participation in the experiment is non-voluntary. If a participant finds employment, either temporary or permanent, this will not affect eligibility the UBI. The tax scheme for the participants in the experiment will be identical to non-participants.

According to the official website for the experiment,

'The basic income experiment seeks answers to the following questions: 1) How could the social security system be redesigned to address the changing nature of work? 2) Can the social security system be reshaped in a way that promotes active participation and gives people a stronger incentive to work? 3) Can bureaucracy be reduced and the complicated benefits system simplified?'[3]

The first and third points reflect widespread concerns about global sociological megatrends. But the second point, with its focus on 'promoting active participation' spells trouble in light of the powerful labourist myths of social democracy. The experiment has been limited to active job seekers, and this has effectively left the back door open for various 'labour market activation' schemes which might tie eligibility criteria (conditionality) back into basic income – eroding its universality.

An earthquake in Finland

The spectre of labourism

The prevalent faith in labourism – transposed into the moral duty of every citizen – stands as the single biggest obstacle to the implementation of a truly *unconditional* UBI. It should come as no surprise, then, that the Sipilä government, in a 'good cop, bad cop' routine, is pushing hard for workfare schemes and tighter benefit conditionality *at the same time* as it is experimenting with UBI.

As long as labourism prevails, all attempts to reform the complex benefit structure towards the key principles of unconditionality and universality are likely to hit an invisible wall. As long as the 'success' of a welfare policy is measured primarily in terms of its effect on work incentives, all other social metrics and moral considerations – of, say, increased freedom for poor people, or increased social equality – are of secondary importance.

Finnish researchers have argued pessimistically that the experiment:

'... is being whittled down before it even properly begins. ... Universal basic income can only succeed if the effort is sustained and widespread – and not available only to the unemployed. The programme should not be intended to force people into low-paying jobs.'[4]

Similar sentiments have been expressed by many critics.[5]

In short, the narrow moral focus on work incentives impoverishes the conversation by excluding relevant theories of justice (including libertarian, egalitarian and humanitarian perspectives). In addition, the narrow pre-selection of the target group excludes many relevant demographics, including the young, old, self-employed, students and entrepreneurs who might theoretically benefit from a UBI. The small sample (2,000), dispersed randomly across a wide population, undermines the effective measurement of chaotic large-scale dynamic effects.

I wish to stress, however, that the quality of the experiment is still comparatively high. The pertinent point of comparison should *not* be any ideal UBI model, or any ideal experimental set-up, but the less-than-ideal reality of the contested political sphere hampered by special interest politics and the chaotic whirlwind of often contradictory policy goals. The Finnish experiment can therefore be favourably compared to similar pilot projects around the world, many of which have also been plagued by poor design or poor data gathering.[6]

At the time of writing, it is too early to estimate the complex long-term impact, scientific and political, of the Finnish experiment. It is easy to jump onto the bandwagon before it has even left the station. Unfortunately many prominent newspapers, who should know better, have already extolled 'findings' as proving that UBI is reducing stress levels among participants.[7] These reports are premature.[8]

The limited scope of the experiment means that it is unlikely to produce uncontested results. Many people are going to read the ambiguous results as tentative confirmation of their biases. Still others will be able to ignore the experimental results altogether due to the experiment's non-ideal parameters.

The main motivations behind the experiment have been political (and not scientific) in nature, and the main ripples are also likely to be political in nature. The end of the experiment coincides roughly with the next general elections in 2019. The current government coalition parties might be able to capitalise on the perceived success of the UBI experiment. The opposition parties, including the Greens and the Left Alliance, are likely to push harder for even more rapid UBI reforms. Nonetheless, the likelihood that the next government of 2019 will proceed with a full implementation of UBI is extremely low due to the institutional constraints of the political system. We are much more likely to see various mixed reforms towards, but falling short of, a true UBI. We are also likely to see efforts to tighten conditionality requirements as part of austerity, and these two parallel developments may fuse into some kind of conditional basic income or 'participation income' schemes.

Outside Finland, the Finnish experiment can serve as a new point of reference for further discussions about welfare. The rather conservative nature of the Finnish experiment is likely

An earthquake in Finland

to prove a talking point for the non-radical wings of the UBI movement. This is a good thing, since big social changes in a social democracy require the co-involvement of moderate political forces who hold the keys to the establishment. For that reason, the political legacy of the Finnish experiment, as a symbolic herald of future reforms, may outlive its narrow scientific usefulness.

An earthquake in Finland

32

Growing a movement: the Canadian context

Roderick Benns and Jenna van Draanen, Canada

'If a wealthy, G7 nation like Canada were to adopt some form of basic income policy, it would surely signal a social economy revolution for the world.'

Every great movement springs from the unmet needs of the people. Every successful movement occurs when those same needs are recognised by a willing faction of innovative policymakers, not afraid to challenge the old ways.

Here, then, is the basic income movement in Canada, on the cusp of convergence of these two truths. On the one hand, a precarious class of people has emerged, made up of lower income workers trapped in part-time work, millennials feeling a sense of career frustration and urgency, and educated professionals trapped in perennial cycles of contract work. The same story plays out in the UK, US, and other western nations. On the other hand, there is growing high level political support across all three levels of Canada's political system – municipal, provincial, and federal – to remedy this through some form of guaranteed minimum income.

A health imperative

Basic income manages to straddle a broad range of critical public policy, and none as important as health. There is strong evidence of its potential benefits from the health sector, and especially from research that demonstrates the impact of the social determinants of health on entire populations. There is also strong support alongside this evidence from many health organisations and health practitioners within local, provincial, and national public health organisations across Canada.

The Alberta and Ontario Public Health Associations have made clear statements of support. A growing number of local health units from municipalities across Canada's largest province, Ontario, have endorsed the concept of a basic income including the Haliburton, Kawartha Pine Ridge, Simcoe Muskoka, and Sudbury District Health Units.[9]

The Association of Local Public Health Agencies and the Ontario Boards of Health have also endorsed basic income and are requesting that the federal ministers across a broad range of government ministries prioritise 'joint federal-consideration and investigation into a basic income guarantee as a policy option for reducing poverty and income insecurity.'[10] Key medical associations in the country have also given support for a basic income along with the Canadian Medical Association.[11]

The concept of a basic income had long been gathering support in Canada and was recommended by a Royal Commission (The Macdonald Commission) in 1985. In 2015-16, a number of provinces indicated their support for local trials, while the Liberal Party, which won the 2016 federal election, passed a resolution in support of the idea.

The provinces show the way

Ontario - Canada's largest province - has led the way, with a roll-out of pilots in three places during 2017. The pilots began in late spring in the city of Hamilton (which will include Brantford and Brant County), and in the northern Ontario city of

Thunder Bay and surrounding area. The third pilot will be in the town of Lindsay, an idyllic centre of 20,000 known for its tourism and surrounding agricultural land. Lindsay's pilot won't start until fall, giving the province time to iron out any wrinkles in the programme.

Out of the 4,000 participants invited to participate, 1,000 are from the Hamilton/Brantford area and another 1,000 from Thunder Bay. However, 2,000 participants will be invited from the smallest centre of Lindsay, making it a vital aspect of the pilot to test behaviours, work patterns, health and mental health outcomes, housing stability, educational attainment, and how the community as a whole may benefit. The pilots in Hamilton and Thunder Bay resemble a randomised controlled trial with participants being randomly invited to participate, and are focused on collecting data on individual-level outcomes. The pilot in Lindsay, on the other hand, is designed to resemble a saturation site with all eligible individuals in Lindsay being invited to participate and data collected to measure community-level changes.

The plan is to invite a mix of low-income people into the programme, such as those who are working but not enough to stay out of poverty, those who are currently on social assistance, and homeless people.

Under the basic income pilot in Ontario – to last three years – eligible participants receive:

- up to C$16,989 per year for a single person, less 50% of any earned income
- up to C$24,027 per year for a couple, less 50% of any earned income
- up to an additional C$6,000 per year for a person with a disability

Quebec is Canada's second largest province (in population, first in area). Its minister of employment and social solidarity, François Blais, wrote a book on basic income called *Ending Poverty: A Basic Income for All Canadians*.[12] The Quebec Liberal government hinted strongly in early 2017 that some form of basic income guarantee was being planned for that year – but likely only for a small portion of the province, at least to begin with. Quebec will likely bypass any pilot or testing of the programme and instead will begin a restrained roll-out of a minimum income programme aimed at lifting the most vulnerable out of poverty.

As at July 2017 there was a power-sharing deal that could transform the political landscape of British Columbia (B.C.), Canada's third-largest province. After the results of a late May election, the New Democratic Party (NDP) and Green Party, combined, have a one-seat majority in the B.C. legislature against the provincial Liberal Party. In an agreed statement of priorities, the NDP and Greens are committed to running a basic income pilot.

The federal level

At the federal level, where Canada's new Liberal Party under Prime Minister Justin Trudeau has embraced a progressive agenda, Jean-Yves Duclos, the Minister of Families, Children and Social Development, has stated that a guaranteed minimum income is a policy worthy of discussion. This opens the door to possible federal involvement. Key senators like Liberal Art Eggleton and his retired counterpart, Conservative Senator Hugh Segal, have also been relentlessly pushing this issue.

In Canada's cities, the political support is significant. It includes big city mayors like Calgary's Mayor Naheed Nenshi, Edmonton's Mayor Don Iveson and Halifax's Mike Savage. In fact, no less than nine provincial and territorial capital leaders support basic income or at least pilot projects, with innumerable smaller city and town mayors across the nation also supporters. They believe — as government leaders who are closest to the people — that a guaranteed income would reduce inequities in their communities, reduce crime, improve health outcomes, and strengthen social cohesion.

At the federal Liberal Party's national convention held in May 2016 in Winnipeg, a resolution was passed that states that the federal Liberals will, in consultation with the provinces, 'develop a poverty reduction strategy aimed at providing a minimum guaranteed income.'

The man who founded Medicare in Canada, Tommy Douglas, nearly lost his leg to amputation when an infection set in. As his many biographers tell, a travelling surgeon agreed to operate for free, as long as his parents allowed his medical students to watch. After several operations, Douglas not only walked again, he never forgot his childhood experience. He resolved that no one should have to pay for necessary medical care. His efforts are now celebrated within Canada's history, for not only did he establish Medicare, he also established democratic socialism here.

That same democratic socialism is on the verge of a massive amplification, should basic income be adopted. As we know from Medicare's historical example, the policy began in Saskatchewan and was quickly adopted by the nation. If even one province in Canada makes this leap then more will follow.

Such a transformation would not end at Canada's borders. If a wealthy, G7 nation like Canada were to adopt some form of basic income policy, it would surely signal a social economy revolution for the world. With the unstoppable forces of globalisation and automation, the pressure and insistence for change is palpable. We now have the willing policymakers. We have the unmet needs of the people, their voices clear.

Change is coming.

Growing a movement: the Canadian context

33

The post social democratic pathway for the 21st century: the Dutch example

Alexander de Roo, The Netherlands

'The rise of the precariat, and the decreased popularity of the two political parties that built the Dutch welfare state, is opening the way for a post social democratic era. Basic income has the strongest card.'

In Western Europe, the 20th century was the century of social democracy; a model where paid work was the central focus, full (male) employment was the norm, and social benefits were conditional. Today, the social democratic model of the welfare state is in deep crisis. It is no longer working, and no longer appealing to the voters. The power of European social democracy has been based on the strength of the union movement. The steady erosion of both the old model of work and of the power of unions over the last 40 years – membership of Dutch unions peaked in the late 1970s – has contributed to the decline of the social democratic movement, but also created opportunities for basic income as a model for a new social contract in the 21st century.

The Social Democratic Party (PvdA) reached an all-time low with 5.8% of the vote in the March 2017 national elections. The Christian Democratic Party (CDA), which also played a crucial role in the build-up of the Dutch welfare state, is also in structural decline. The popularity of the CDA in general elections has declined from an absolute majority in the 1950s to 12.4% in 2017. In the general elections in 2006, the Christian Democratic and Social Democratic parties together secured 46% of the vote. In March 2017, their combined share had fallen to 18%, and the election was won by Mark Rutte: Prime Minister since October 2010 and the leader of the right-of-centre People's Party for Freedom and Democracy.

These profound political trends have been accompanied by powerful changes in the nature of work in the Netherlands. Today, a fifth of the Dutch workforce – 2 million people – have a flexible contract, while 1 million are self-employed. The nation is witnessing an increase in the number of flexible jobs and a decline in security and the regularity of work. Similar trends have been occurring across the European continent. Because of these shifts, the size of the Dutch precariat has been estimated at 4 million (roughly 40% of the population), while the unions are trying to convince politicians to restore the old model of stable, regulated jobs through legislation.

The rise of the precariat, and the decreased popularity of the two political parties that built the Dutch welfare state, is opening the way for a post social democratic era. Basic income has the strongest card.

In contrast to the fierce debate about basic income in the Netherlands in the 1980s and 1990s, large parts of the Dutch population are now receptive to the idea. This is because the present welfare system is – in the eyes of the population – no longer worth fighting for.

The Dutch branch of BIEN (the global Basic Income Earth Network) – de Vereniging Basisinkomen – was founded in 1989. The Dutch Social Democratic party almost adopted basic income in its national election programme in 1993. In 1994 there was even a discussion in the national government when Hans Weijers, the Minister of Economic Affairs (D66, left-wing liberals), and Gerrit Zalm, Minister of Finance (VVD, right-wing liberals), argued in favour of a basic income. In the event, Prime Minister Wim Kok (Social Democrats) argued that the idea was too early and would need to wait another 30 years. A public opinion survey by the Social and Cultural Planning Bureau in 1993 showed that only 19% favoured a partial basic income. The debate about basic income in the Netherlands faded away in the early years of the new millennium as a result of the economic upswing, but made a strong comeback in the changed economic and political landscape from 2008. The current debate has become much more intense and pragmatic than 25 years ago. With the rise of economic insecurity, there is also a growing awareness of the urgent need for a new approach to social security among the general public.

In a 2016 national poll,[13] 40% of the Dutch population voted in favour of a basic income, 45% voted against and 15% were undecided. A majority of voters for the left-of-centre parties were in favour: 60% of Greens, and 53% of Social Democrats. Left-wing liberals were divided: 44% in favour and 45% against. Supporters of the populist right-wing Freedom Party of Geert Wilders were also divided. A 2017 poll resulted in 51% in favour and 49% against.[14]

In the 2017 national election campaign, basic income advocates managed to persuade the left-wing liberal party (D66) and the Green Party to take a more positive stand on basic income in their manifestos. Most other political parties oppose basic income, some in principle (the right-wing liberals VVD and far left SP), and others because they see it as too expensive (Social and Christian Democrats). The pensioner party – 50Plus – has a study group on basic income while, overall, parties representing 30% of the electorate were positive about basic income in their manifestos. Compared with virtually no attention at all in the 2012 elections, that is a huge jump.

My personal experience, when handing out our basic income flyers to the general public, is that half of the people take them and react positively, while the other half tend to ignore us. On one occasion, a young couple passed by me arm-in-arm. The young male indicated he was not interested, but the young female left her boyfriend and walked back to take a leaflet! We have lively discussions with the general public. Even young people under 25 know very well what a basic income is.

The comeback of the basic income idea in the Dutch debate has been boosted by a book from the young historian Rutger Bregman, *Free Money for Everyone*, published in September 2014, and a couple of national television documentaries. Bregman's book was published in English - *Utopia for Realists* - in 2017. The topic of basic income also gets regular attention on television, radio, the internet and in newspapers.

The Dutch pilots

In the Netherlands, the debate about launching local pilots began in 2015. In 2016, legislation allowed municipalities, in principle, to experiment with innovative social policies. Nineteen municipalities declared they would like to undertake a basic income pilot. Utrecht, Groningen, Tilburg and Wageningen were the first in the ring, and, with others, began discussions about the exact rules of such pilots with the state Secretary of Social Affairs and Employment. It was hoped that, with the right sort of design, the pilots would answer several questions, including:

- Will people become more active in the labour market if they are free of conditions, in comparison with the present situation, where they have to apply for jobs and are closely monitored?
- Will people become more autonomous?
- Will they become healthier?
- Will they participate sooner in paid work if they are allowed to earn some extra money on top of their allowance?

The pilots were expected to begin in early 2017, but the central government was lukewarm and very slow to give a final green light. Before the election in March 2017, 15 of the 17 political groupings in Parliament were willing to give the go-ahead for the experiments, but the biggest partner in the coalition government - VVD, the right-wing liberal party - was opposed. This resulted in long delays and very stringent conditions in the design of the pilots before the government would allow the municipalities to proceed.

At the beginning of July 2017 after two years of discussion, five municipalities (Groningen, Tilburg, Deventer, Nijmegen and Wageningen) were finally given the go-ahead, and will start their two year experiments in the fall of 2017. Amsterdam and Utrecht were told by the government to change their local regulations to add an element of workfare, before their pilots can start. Amsterdam decided to ignore the government and to start their pilot in September without government approval. The council of Utrecht will decide in September whether to follow the Amsterdam example or change their local regulation in order to start their experiment.

As social science critics of the proposed schemes have emphasised, the pilots have not been designed to test a universal and fully unconditional basic income.[15] First, the population of the experiment is not 'universal'. Participants will be selected from current welfare recipients with the pilot designed to test the effects on participation in labour markets when the unemployed are freed from obligations and given unconditional welfare benefits (this is similar to the approach of the Finnish experiment, launched on 1 January 2017 – see Chapter 31). Secondly, the benefit will remain means-tested and household-based (rather than individual-based), in both respects very different from a full universal scheme.

Indeed, proponents of the Dutch experiments have avoided the use of the term 'basic income' ('basisinkomen' in Dutch), with researchers in Utrecht calling their proposed experiment by the name 'Weten Wat Werkt' ('Know What Works'). Despite the sharp differences of view about the merits of their design, there is still hope that the Dutch experiments may turn out to be a step toward a fully-fledged basic income. At least basic income will remain in the public discussion because of these experiments.

34

The California experiment

Elizabeth Rhodes,
Y Combinator Research, USA

'This project is the first step toward defining a new social contract for the 21st century.'

Public interest in basic income has skyrocketed as many have realised that current social spending fails to adequately meet people's needs and prepare them for rapid changes in the labour market. Despite the buzz, no researchers have taken on the challenge of exploring what a basic income really means for individuals in the US.

Y Combinator Research (YCR) is a non-profit research organisation established to explore big ideas to address long-term, societal-level problems. YCR announced its intention to conduct a basic income study in January 2016 and has since hired researchers and partnered with academics at Stanford and the University of Michigan. YCR is uniquely positioned to bring together leading researchers and leverage the technical expertise, ingenuity, and operational strengths of Silicon Valley. This project is the first step toward defining a new social contract for the 21st century.

Motivation

In the US, extreme poverty has dramatically increased, the middle class is shrinking, and employment and incomes have become more volatile and unpredictable.[16] The technological and economic forces that contribute to these trends are unlikely to subside, and existing social programmes have proven insufficient to stem them.

For the poor, the need to make ends meet today, tomorrow, and next month means they can't embrace opportunities that lead to long-term economic security. They don't have the freedom to make investments in education or training, take risks that those with financial or family support often take for granted, or decide how to use public assistance to meet their specific needs.

The patchwork of programmes comprising the safety net is complex, difficult to navigate, and costly to administer. Expenditures on these programmes continue to increase but millions of Americans remain in poverty.[17] Proposals to improve these programmes only tinker around the edges, acting as band-aids rather than sustainable solutions. YCR aims to explore an alternative approach that empowers individuals to realise their potential. Basic income could change the trajectory of people's lives. It could provide a safety net for young adults as they transition from school to work, enable individuals to change careers or start a new business, or allow them to care for a child or elderly relative.

Basic income could also relieve poverty. Research suggests that negative economic, social, and psychological feedback loops keep individuals without a steady income 'trapped' in poverty. Unconditional cash transfers seek to break these loops, and a new wave of rigorous studies in developing countries affirms this potential. Basic income could streamline the social safety net, remove a myriad of work disincentives, and spark entrepreneurship.

This idea garners support across the political spectrum. Libertarians argue that basic income could reform an inefficient and ineffective welfare state. Anti-poverty advocates believe basic income is the simplest plan to end poverty. Tech leaders such as Mark Zuckerberg of Facebook, Elon Musk, founder and CEO at Space Exploration Technologies, SpaceX, and Sam Altman, the president of start-up accelerator Y Combinator, have advocated for this research, as they've personally witnessed automation's potential to disrupt work. Others—on left and right—remain sceptical, raising concerns about the cost or the psychological and existential consequences for recipients.

Despite all the debate, the arguments for and against basic income are largely theoretical or ideological. The magnitude of the costs and benefits in the US context are unclear. The lack of data and experience impedes rigorous policy analyses and exacerbates the political challenge for basic income advocates.

The gold standard for understanding a new social policy is a randomised controlled trial (RCT). By comparing a group of people who receive a basic income to an otherwise identical group of people who do not, researchers can isolate and quantify the effects of a basic income.

In early September 2016 YCR launched the first small wave of a pilot study in Oakland, CA, that ran for one year. Researchers do not expect to generate meaningful insight into research questions with the pilot, as the sample will be far too small and the time horizon too short to simulate the expectation of long-term economic security. Instead, they are using the pilot to test payment mechanisms and other logistics; refine intermediate and final outcome measures; test data collection instruments and methodology; develop strategies for limiting attrition in the control group; and determine whether the experimental protocol is likely to generate insight into the research questions.

In 2018, YCR plans to launch a larger, longer-term RCT. It will randomly select 3,000 individuals across two US states to participate in the study: 1,000 will receive $1,000 per month for 3 or 5 years, and 2,000 will serve as a control group for comparison. Individuals between the ages of 21 and 40 whose total household income does not exceed the area median income for their county of residence are eligible to participate in the study. The sample will be stratified to ensure representation

The California experiment

across several dimensions, including race and ethnicity, gender, and income. Participants will be given a pre-loaded debit card and online banking account at enrolment, and monthly basic income and survey incentive payments will be deposited into these accounts. Altman has said he is less interested in the impact on employment, than on people's choices in response to a guaranteed income: 'Do people sit around and play video games, or do they create new things?' Do they 'without the fear of not being able to eat, accomplish far more and benefit society far more?'[18]

Researchers will conduct extensive quantitative measurement of outcomes related to individuals' economic, social, and physiological self-sufficiency and wellbeing. They will also gather data on how individuals use their time and money, as well as how their receipt of a basic income impacts their children and those in their networks. To ensure that measurement strategies are accurate and reflect the latest research, YCR is partnering with state and local agencies to collect objective administrative outcomes and working with leading experts in economics, medicine, and other fields. Collecting data on these outcomes will help researchers learn how this basic level of economic security helps people cope—and even thrive—in the midst of volatility and uncertainty.

YCR also plans to conduct regular in-depth interviews with a subset of participants to better understand how a basic income influences people's lives. Documenting individuals' experiences, their decision-making processes, and the constraints they face will help researchers answer fundamental questions about basic income and advance the debate about social spending and the future of work.

35

'Eight': the Ugandan pilot

Steven Janssens, Eight, Belgium

'There will be positive effects on the local economy and businesses, an increase in local, small companies being set up. Overall, I think we will see a more solid society and more solidarity. During the first seven months of the project, the early signs are that these predictions are being realised, and indeed, exceeding expectations.'

I came up with the idea of Eight, a small basic income pilot in Uganda, via my work as a filmmaker in the developing world. I had often wondered how it is possible to have so many NGOs with so many Jeeps, expensive equipment and well-paid staff, when the villages they're working in are so poor that the entire population could be fed for weeks on these outlays. It was this that led me to the idea of giving everyone in a particular area a basic income.

I was also passionate about levels of inequality, with a few powerful people routinely able take a lot from the natural world, like oil and other resources, that should belong to everyone and be naturally shared. We live in a world in which we could easily afford to give a basic income to everyone. It makes no sense to me that some people can buy ten helicopters, while others are dying because of a lack of food. A basic income would contribute to a more equal world – it is not left or right, it is not socialist or communist, it's a new vision. Because it's saying 'look, you get money and you can do with it whatever you want', basic income is right/liberal in some ways, but it's also left because it is about creating greater equality of chances and outcomes, a more equal world.

What is Eight?

The idea behind Eight, a not-for-profit organisation which we started in late 2015, is to give everyone in a small village a monthly basic income, enough to live a basic life on. The pilot began in January 2017 and is to last two years. We chose to run the pilot in rural Uganda because I have spent a lot of time in Uganda, my wife is Ugandan, and it is affordable. Doing a pilot of this type in the west would simply be unaffordable for a small crowd-funded charity. The trial is not state funded – it is independent and private. It has been funded by donations from around the world, starting with our own inner circle. By running the pilot in this way rather than as a government funded project, we are able to avoid external influence and to keep full control.

My colleague and co-founder of Eight, Maarten Goethals, left his job in an NGO five years ago and became an independent consultant for NGOs, also in Uganda. Together we know the country, and have a strong network there, making it easy to build cooperation and to finance the project.

As well as my wife, a social scientist, others involved in the project are a lawyer and a small film-crew. It's really a cooperation between Belgium and Uganda!

Although Uganda was an obvious starting point for us, choosing the village for the pilot was an involved project in itself. We wanted the pilot to be controlled and to affect a whole community, so it was important to find a small, rural village where we could afford to pay every adult using donations. For the moment, the pilot project is completely funded for two years. We hope to scale up our intervention to ten villages in 2020.

The project is called 'Eight' because €8 is a monthly basic income for a child and €16 is a monthly basic income for an adult in this particular region of Uganda. This is based on poverty levels, using a combination of parameters necessary for survival.[19] It's a basic income, just enough to provide food and basic needs, but not luxuries. The shape of the number '8' shows infinity and continuity, and the pronunciation of 'Eight' is very similar to 'Aid'.

So each adult and child (through the carer) in a village of 58 adults and 88 children in the Fort Portal region of rural Uganda has been receiving an unconditional basic income. There are no restrictions or guidelines on what can be done with the cash transfer. The only criteria for eligibility is that the adult lives in or owns land in the village at the time of registration, and is 18 years or older. In the first month, we gave participants cash in envelopes as some are not used to mobile phones. Since then the payments have been via mobile phones as the most secure way to transfer the money. Along with the first payment, we gave mobile money training to the illiterate and those with no experience of mobile phones.

We have a strong link with two partnering universities (Ghent and Antwerp) that will undertake an independent evaluation, and help us with our plans for the future upscaling of the project in a scientific way. We are making a documentary showing the impact of the experiment which we hope will be finished by 2019. Different versions – webisodes and longer episodes – can be seen on www.villageone.film.

The likely impact

In line with the findings of earlier studies, we are expecting to see many positive outcomes for both individuals and the village as a whole. Providing an income floor and taking people out of the poverty trap is likely to have a real effect. Almost every child will now be able to afford school fees. There will be improved family planning, thus reducing child birth among the young. The long-term effects can include controlled world population growth – it is statistically proven that if you save poor children, you stop population growth.[20]

Healthcare will improve, so that people don't die of a simple illness, but instead can pay the fees to see a doctor and don't have to sell their goat to do so.

There will be positive effects on the local economy and businesses, an increase in local, small companies being set up. Overall, I think we will see a more solid society and more solidarity. During the first seven months of the project, the early signs are that these predictions are being realised and, indeed, exceeding expectations. The villagers are also uniting together to save money. That gives them the opportunity to make larger investments (for example in a cow or a roof). We are also seeing small community projects coming together to improve the lives of all the people in the village.

In terms of work incentives, our belief is that when people get the opportunity to do something productive, most people are going to take it. Of course some people will do less and some will simply stay the same. But I think a basic income will empower most people to have a new direction, to do something that they really want. I am convinced that it will work.

We see this as a pilot project. As it grows and we get more donations, we hope that Eight will become a bigger movement and community. The pilot is just the start. If the model is successful and we can raise sufficient money we'd like to roll out a basic income to multiple villages. We also hope to show that the results of the Ugandan trial would be relevant and applicable to wealthy, developed countries. Additionally, the project is, in itself, a way of exploring alternative models of development aid. If you calculate all development money that is given by western countries to Uganda, and you divide by all inhabitants, you almost have enough for a basic income for every Ugandan.[21]

36

The Kenyan experiment

GiveDirectly, Kenya

'Our pilot will be the largest experiment of a basic income in history, with 6,000 people in 40 communities receiving a basic income for more than a decade, and more than 16,000 people receiving some type of cash transfer.'

The US-based non-governmental organisation, GiveDirectly, is among the leaders of the cash transfer movement, and the first non-profit organisation devoted exclusively to enabling funders to send money directly to the extreme poor. From its roots in Kenya, GiveDirectly has grown across East Africa while driving public debate about the role cash transfers should play. Rigorous experimental evidence has played a key role in this growth: GiveDirectly was founded in light of the strong evidence that cash transfers were working, and has also conducted a number of randomised controlled trials which have further strengthened that evidence base. These evaluations have shown that such transfers lead to a host of positive impacts, from higher living standards to greater food security and even improved psychological well-being.[22] In addition, old concerns – that the poor would abuse transfers on alcohol, for example, or stop working – have not been borne out in the data.

We are tremendously excited to be launching our basic income initiative, which represents both a major new chapter in our history and a continuation of the principles we have stood for from the beginning. For context, essentially every dollar we have delivered to date has been part of a short-term or 'lump-sum' transfer, an immediate transfer of capital which recipients are then free to use or invest as they please. We think this approach makes sense given the evidence that the poor often have access to investment opportunities with very high rates of return: rather than keep the money in our accounts, we prefer to move it out as quickly as possible. Basic income is if anything the exact opposite approach to designing transfers, since it commits to providing small payments in perpetuity.

But we believe that today's global conversation about basic income represents a unique opportunity. Opinions are incredibly polarised, from sceptics who call basic income 'a senseless act of preemptive self-sabotage' to optimists calling it 'to the 21st century what civil and political rights were to the 20th.' And the debate spans the globe, from wealthy countries considering basic income as a response to automation and job loss to lower-income countries like India considering it as a tool for eliminating extreme poverty. We think it is critical that issues of this enormity are debated in the context of hard facts. And since generating hard facts about cash transfers is one of our core competencies, we decided to take the plunge.

The basic income initiative we are running in Kenya is ambitious on many dimensions. It will be the largest (to our knowledge), with 6,000 people receiving long-term basic income support and a total of 16,000 people receiving some form of cash transfer. It will be the longest, again to our knowledge, with participants in the long-term arm receiving a commitment to transfers lasting over a decade. This is critical as it will allow us to measure not just the effects of more cash on hand, but also the effects of the promise of future economic security – something that short-term pilots cannot capture. And it will be the first initiative randomised at the community level, which will allow us to measure not only how individual lives change but also how entire communities (here, villages) respond to universal basic income. The specific study arms include a long-term basic income arm made up of 40 villages with 6,000 recipients receiving $0.75 per adult per day ($22 per month) for 12 years; a short-term basic income arm made up of 80 villages with recipients receiving the same monthly amount, but for 2 years; and a control arm made up of 100 villages not receiving cash transfers. Comparing the first and second groups of villages will shed light on how important the guarantee of future transfers is for outcomes today (for example, taking a risk like starting a business), while the comparison between the first and third groups will let us measure the overall impact of a UBI guarantee.

The initiative itself will be paired with rigorous evaluation led by leading economic researchers. Along with GiveDirectly's co-founders Michael Faye and Paul Niehaus, the study is led by Professors Abhijit Banerjee (MIT, co-founder of the Jameel Poverty Action Lab), Tavneet Suri (MIT) and Alan Krueger (Princeton, former chairman of the Council of Economic Advisors). An independent contractor, Innovations for Poverty Action (IPA), will conduct research surveying, and data collection and analysis plans will be pre-specified and published to ensure the integrity of inferences from the results.

The study will examine impacts on a wide range of outcomes, reflecting the fact that a basic income is likely to affect every aspect of recipient's lives. In addition to standard economic outcomes (income, expenditure, assets) we will examine effects on everything from time use (Do people go back to school? Quit their jobs? Get involved in community activities?) to risk-taking behaviours (Do they migrate? Start businesses?) to gender relations (Do women become more empowered?) to aspirations and life outlook. While the transfers will last for 12 years, we expect to begin measuring effects within the first year or two, enabling us to see how the guarantee of a basic income in the future affects the behaviour and well-being of recipients today.

With several other basic income pilots now launched around the globe, this is an exciting moment both for the idea and for the evidence-based policy movement more broadly. Potentially game-changing ideas like basic income deserve rigorous testing; we're excited to be part of the coalition that is making it happen.

37

Brazil: a basic income experiment as a citizen-to-citizen project

Bruna Augusto and
Marcus Brancaglione, Brazil

'A basic income may be the cheapest and most effective solution for increasing the social capital and the common good of a neighbourhood'

Brazil's ReCivitas Institute, founded in 2006, is a non-profit, non-governmental organisation that develops social projects with the goal of promoting free enterprise, empowerment and an emancipated citizenry. Among these projects is the Quatinga Velho basic income experiment. This currently runs on the 'Basic Income Startup model', the virtual platform for citizen's governance and digital direct democracy.[23]

The Basic Income social project in Quatinga Velho started in October 2008. The first experimental phase lasted from October 2008 to May 2015. The second and current phase – 'Basic Income Startup' – began in January 2016 and is designed to be permanent.

Phase 1: 2008–15

During the period up to 2015, we maintained a monthly payment of an unconditional basic income of 30 reais (US$12) to residents of Vila de Quatinga Velho, São Paulo, Brazil. The first payment was given in person to 27 people and was funded by a donation from the project administrators. In the first six months, after building community trust, enrolment reached 100 people and remained around that figure until the project ended. During this phase, weekly visits were made to the participants' homes and monthly assemblies were held during which participants self-managed the project, both through collective decision-making about issues relating to the project and to vote on proposals for onboarding new residents.

Since the beginning the project has been independent, driven by volunteer effort, without any corporate or governmental sponsorship. Online fundraising campaigns were maintained throughout the project. All donations were fully allocated to basic income payments. Operational costs were paid by the project coordinators who worked as unpaid volunteers.

Throughout, we collected data and informed participants about the project's progress through informal conversation. To encourage support and to teach children about the concept of basic income, a mobile book and toy library was assembled. There were visits from scholars and students from foreign universities which, together with ReCivitas' own reports, compose the record of analyses and results collected through this period. The data and results of the project were included in accounting reports and marketing materials for the project, which helped in the fundraising effort. Despite this, resources were insufficient to continue Phase 1.

Phase 2: 2016–present

After an hiatus in payments of one year, the project resumed in 2016 with a new, self-sustaining funding model. During this time, funds were raised and paid into a Guarantor Fund which earns a savings account interest rate and, from that interest, basic income payments are made.

By the summer of 2017, there was enough funding to pay 19 participants R$40 (US$14) a month, guaranteed for life (each payment requires €1,000 to be raised for the Guarantor Fund). The operational model has changed. In the first phase, most residents did not have bank accounts or internet-enabled cellphones, whereas now all payments are made by electronic transfer and all communications are electronic. Participants also make voluntary contributions to the Guarantor Fund, and the rates of contribution are determined by the participants themselves. Thus, in the long term, the participants will be able to pay for their own basic income and the capital currently allocated to pay for their basic income may be used to pay a basic income to people in other places.

We continue to seek donations and, when the Guarantor Fund allows, a self-sustaining basic income payment to a new person can be started. In Phase 2, a major hurdle has been overcome in that the project is not at risk of ending due to a lack of funds; instead, it is fundraising to permanently reach more people, guaranteeing them a basic income payment for life.

Why Quatinga Velho?

We were looking for a community in which the level of resources at our disposal would be sufficient to begin the project, and not just for an isolated community, but one that was practically abandoned by the government. This would ensure that the data and the results would not be affected by other governmental programmes, and that the government would not interfere with the project's day-to-day activities. So we aimed for an isolated place that presented the lowest possible cost of living, thus enabling the payments we could afford to go further.

The first phase – over five years – was sufficient time for independent studies to assess the project's impact and the development of social capital. As shown in Figure 37.1, participants used their basic income on the most basic purchases,

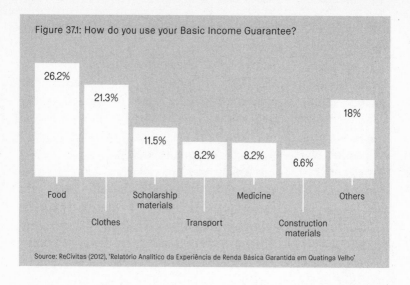

Figure 37.1: How do you use your Basic Income Guarantee?

Source: ReCivitas (2012), 'Relatório Analítico da Experiência de Renda Básica Garantida em Quatinga Velho'

such as food, doctor visits and medicine, construction material for homes and school supplies. Some families started financial planning and micro-businesses selling bread or cake, or purchased chickens to sell eggs, building the local economy. Others used the resources to seek out jobs in other localities.

As shown in Figure 37.2, most families enjoyed an increase in their ability to guarantee basic needs for themselves and their family.

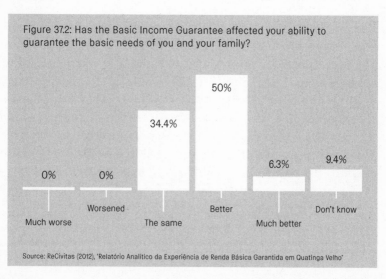

Figure 37.2: Has the Basic Income Guarantee affected your ability to guarantee the basic needs of you and your family?

Source: ReCivitas (2012), 'Relatório Analítico da Experiência de Renda Básica Garantida em Quatinga Velho'

Brazil: a basic income experiment as a citizen-to-citizen project

We realised that people started talking about the future of their children with increased frequency and with increased hope for opportunities. The project resulted in a gradual liberation of people from a state of passivity towards their life circumstances, enabling them to consider and design their own paths in life. We believe that this is one of the most important results for human development. We found that basic income impacted not only on current emergencies, but on the construction of the future. A majority – 59% – said that the basic income helped 'a little bit' and 13% 'a lot' with shaping their futures.

The evidence of the Quatinga Velho experiment is that, by giving people resources, they are incentivised to make good use of them and to take advantage of a wider array of choices that were previously inaccessible. Funds given unconditionally and without expectations work as an expression of trust, stimulating a feeling of reciprocity to the act itself. In conversations with all participants they express a clear need to explain and to show how well they are applying the resources they receive. This is not about showing how good they are at it, but as a gesture of reciprocity to the trust they received in the process, both from ReCivitas and from the community itself.

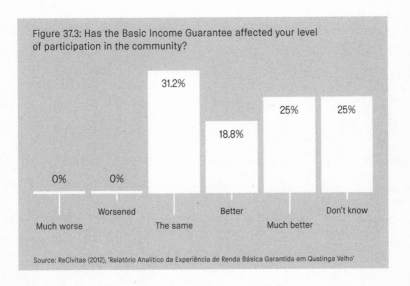

Figure 37.3: Has the Basic Income Guarantee affected your level of participation in the community?

Source: ReCivitas (2012), 'Relatório Analítico da Experiência de Renda Básica Garantida em Quatinga Velho'

Brazil: a basic income experiment as a citizen-to-citizen project

The evidence from the project is that a basic income may be the cheapest and most effective solution for increasing the social capital and the common good of a neighbourhood. Indeed, as shown in Figure 37.3, for 44% of participants, the basic income raised their level of participation in the community.

The future

Thanks to the Basic Income Startup model, we are able to dedicate ourselves to fundraising and forming partnerships, aimed at expanding the project to reach more people. The model allows for a gradual and sustained expansion of participants, as funds increase. What we now lack is funding. In this way, we share the same fate as the people we serve, those that live in the peripheries: like them, we have everything we need to grow and to be able to contribute more to the world, except for capital.

Perhaps we will need a third phase. Maybe we need to issue our own currencies, our own money. But we will not skip steps. We will see. The experience itself will tell us where we need to go.

PART VI: THE WAY FORWARD

38

Building momentum

Amy Downes and Stewart Lansley, UK

The last few years have seen what the Paris-based OECD has called a 'remarkable' jump in interest in a universal basic income.[1] Pilots, of varying forms and ambition, some funded by national governments and others by crowd-funding charities (such as Eight and GiveDirectly) and wealthy industrialists (such as those at Y Combinator), are under way in a mix of developed and developing countries. While the full impact of these pilots will not be known for some years, they are having a galvanising effect on the UBI debate. The pilots – and more may follow – represent, in themselves, a remarkable global social experiment. As well as taking place, more or less simultaneously, in a diversity of nations and continents, they are well constructed, will offer significant evidence on the potential impact of different models of UBI and are being very closely observed.

What binds supporters of a basic income, and many of the contributions in this book, is its potential to plug some of the holes in existing systems of social security, and to offer greater social protection in an era of growing work insecurity and risk. But a UBI also does much more than this. Many contributors – from Insead's Eduardo Rodriguez-Montemayor in Chapter 2 to The Leap Manifesto's Avi Lewis and Katie McKenna in Chapter 12 – talk of how, by encouraging greater choice and strengthening labour's bargaining power, a UBI would empower citizens and help meet growing public demands for a fairer society. In Chapter 23, Philippe Van Parijs argues that a UBI's guaranteed income floor – below which no-one would fall – should be central to the renewal of social democracy.

Nevertheless, a UBI is not, as one contributor puts it, 'a magical solution'. It will help deal with some of the fault lines of today's economic and social systems, but not all. It is therefore important, as several contributors have cautioned, that the case for UBI is not overstated, and that it is clear that a UBI would need to be accompanied by other reforms targeted at issues like work insecurity, stagnant and falling wages, and the growing concentration of wealth ownership. There are also many different models of a UBI, while actual schemes would need to be tailored to different tax systems, social cultures and stages of development. What works for one country might not for another.

While interest has been building, the nature of the debate has been evolving from questions of desirability to those of feasibility and implementation. There is a growing acceptance – even among the most committed of advocates – that a big bang approach that sweeps away large parts of existing systems of social security cannot be made to work. As examined in Chapters 29 and 30, successful implementation would require an incremental and staged approach to reform. In their recent book, *Basic Income,* the leading advocates, Philippe Van Parijs and Yannick Vanderborght, favour what they call a 'partial' scheme and a 'gradual approach'.[2] Others have urged policymakers 'to proceed with caution'.[3] At least in the medium term, a UBI would have to be grafted onto the existing system, with new unconditional benefits sitting beside existing means-tested and social insurance schemes, rather than replacing them entirely.

The world is now feeling its way towards the future. Whether a UBI plays a central role in this future remains unclear. The idea is gaining a political foothold, and more converts, but remains controversial. While a number of pilots are under way, and others are being discussed, there is little immediate prospect of expansion in the membership of the existing 'basic income club'. The interest now lies in the trials and what they will reveal about the impact of different models of UBI and wider issues of implementation.

Although the pace has been set by those countries initiating trials, the debate has been spreading across nations. In France a 2016 parliamentary commission recommended the testing of a basic income, and the idea was promoted by some 2017 presidential candidates. There have been a number of detailed country studies, including in South Africa, Germany, Australia, New Zealand, Hungary and the UK. In part because of the positive outcome of the 2009–13 Indian trial – outlined in Chapter 26 – Indian politicians are now looking seriously at how a scheme might be introduced.[4]

The experience of countries such as Finland and the Netherlands shows that even reaching the pilot stage requires sustained groundwork. The current trials would not have happened without years of painstaking campaigning by activists, securing press and media interest and building a national debate. In Finland the interest began in the 1980s, and as Otto Lehto discusses in Chapter 31, the current trial is the outcome of 'long-term pressure from civil society'. In the Netherlands, Alexander de Roo (in Chapter 33) explains how an extended public debate, accompanied by television programmes and films, and fuelled by a growing disillusion with the present welfare system, has made 'large parts of the Dutch population now receptive to the idea'.

In the UK, the idea has gained firm support from organisations as diverse as the influential Royal Society of Arts and the Compass pressure group, while the pro-market think-tank, the Adam Smith Institute, has called for the introduction of a negative income tax to replace a range of means-tested benefits.[5] There have been a number of detailed simulations of its feasibility and how it might work in practice, while both the UK Parliament's Work and Pensions Select Committee and the Scottish Parliament's Social Security Committee have conducted inquiries.[6]

The debate in the UK is most advanced in Scotland, where there is growing pressure to extend the list of experiments and launch a pilot. Nevertheless, as Annie Miller explains in Chapter 27, despite the undoubted Scottish momentum, and the commitment of the Scottish government to fund research into the idea, much more preparatory work is needed before a pilot becomes a serious possibility, and Miller sets out the kind of detailed planning that would be needed before a pilot could be launched.

The introduction of a UK UBI would involve a major transformation in the nature of social protection, the character of the tax/benefit system and the pattern of winners and losers. There would be significant implications for the nature and extent of redistribution, the pattern of work incentives and personal choices. A reform as profound as this could not take place without a full national debate and the emergence of clear public consensus. Most other great and long lasting social reforms – from universal suffrage to the building of the post-war welfare state – had to be fought for and involved years of policy analysis, campaigning and the building of mass public support: the 1942 Beveridge white paper, *Social Insurance and Allied Services*, for example, sold half a million copies.

As Peter Beresford argues in Chapter 20, a UBI cannot simply be imposed from the top, as has happened, for example, with universal credit. Such a fundamental change depends on a 'move from paternalism to participation' and ensuring that the idea 'has involved, engaged and drawn on the diversity of people it is meant to benefit.' In Chapter 10, Anthony Painter writes that a campaign for a UBI would need

> 'A pluralistic movement that reaches across political, ideological and interest divides. The best thing that those who consider basic income to be essential can do is widen the tent. That means being open, welcoming, accepting of well-considered criticism and reaching out.'

Widening the tent requires an open and welcoming debate, and heeding the important warnings made by progressive opponents of a UBI set out in Part III.

Progress will also depend on building a cross-party consensus and the UK is a long way from that. While the Greens are strongly committed, and the Scottish National Party is inching towards support, the Conservative Party has shown little interest in the idea. Vince Cable, the leader of the UK Liberal/Democrats is against, but 60% of party members are for.[7] Labour is also divided. Despite the powerful case made in Chapter 16 by Labour MP Jonathan Reynolds, other Labour figures are opposed.[8]

But although there may be some way to go before another nation bites the bullet, there is considerable momentum behind a basic income. The idea is capturing imaginations across a great diversity of nations, and with the emergence of national campaigns, its support base is growing. Former doubters, such as Ruth Lister CBE (Chapter 9), have signed up to the idea while other recent recruits include the 2010 Nobel laureates in economics, MIT's Peter Diamond and LSE's Sir Christopher Pissarides.[9] This current wave of interest, the fourth over the last century, feels more grounded than the earlier phases, and significantly, more global. In Malcolm Torry's phrase (Chapter 24), there are no signs that the current wave of interest is about to 'subside', as was the case in the earlier ones.

Citizens across nations are losing patience with existing systems of social protection, with pressure mounting on national governments to build a more robust safety net. There is growing concern with inequality and the future of work. People want better choices. Although the case for a UBI has been driven by the promise of greater security for households, it has the potential to contribute to other key progressive goals from greater social justice to the encouragement of more active social participation. As Roope Mokka and Katariina Rantanen from Demos Helsinki argue in Chapter 11, a UBI for the post-industrial age offers much more than a simple 'employment fix' and could 'help to create no less than a shared political vision for a future society'.

Notes

Introduction

1. Browne, J. and Hood, H. (2012) 'A Survey of the UK Benefit System', *IFS Briefing Note BN13,* London, Institute for Fiscal Studies.
2. Tridimas, G. (2013) 'Homo Oeconomicus in Ancient Athens: Silver Bonanza and the Choice to Build a Navy', *Homo Oeconomicus,* 30(4), pp 435–58.
3. Paine, T. (1795) 'Agrarian Justice' in *Common Sense and Other Writings,* New York: Barnes and Noble, pp 332–6.
4. For more on the recent history, see Standing, G. (2017) *Basic Income: And How We Can Make it Happen,* London: Penguin, pp 9–18; and 'History of basic income', BIEN, basicincome.org/basic-income/history.
5. Lansley, S. (2016) *A Sharing Economy: How Social Wealth Funds Can Tackle Inequality and Help Balance the Books,* Bristol: Policy Press, Chapter 4.
6. Tabatabai, H. (2011) 'The basic income road to reforming Iran's price subsidies', *Basic Income Studies,* 6(1), pp 1–24.
7. Since 2013, additional tax has been charged on taxpayers earning over £50,000 living in households that receive child benefit – the High Income Child Benefit Charge – aimed at clawing back child benefit from higher income households.
8. See, for example, Lawrence, M. (2016) *Future Proof, the economy in the 2020s.* London: Institute for Public Policy Research (IPPR).
9. See, for example, Gordon, D.J. (2016) *The Rise and Fall of American Growth,* Princeton University Press.
10. According to a recent report by Accenture and Frontier Economics, automation could raise the annual growth rate of gross value added (a close approximation of GDP) by 4.6% in US, 3.9% in UK, and 2.7% in Japan, newsroom.accenture.com/subjects/technology/artificial-intelligence-poised-to-double-annual-economic-growth-rate-in-12-developed-economies-and-boost-labor-productivity-by-up-to-40-percent-by-2035-according-to-new-research-by-accenture.htm.
11. Quoted in Van Parijs, P. and Sanderborght, Y. (2017) *Basic Income: A Radical Proposal for a Free Society and a Sane Economy,* Cambridge, MA: Harvard University Press, p 79.

[12] 'A post-work economy of robots and machines is a bad Utopia for the left', *The Conversation*, theconversation.com/a-post-work-economy-of-robots-and-machines-is-a-bad-utopia-for-the-left-59134.

[13] Meade, J. (1989) *Agathotopia: The Economics of Partnership*, Aberdeen: Aberdeen University Press.

[14] See, for example, Lansley (2016), and Boyce, J.K. and Barnes, P. (2016) 'How to Pay for Universal Basic Income', Evonomics, evonomics.com/how-to-pay-for-universal-basic-income.

[15] Murray, C. (2008) 'Guaranteed Income as a Replacement for the Welfare State', *Basic Income Studies*, 3(2).

[16] McFarland, K. (2017) 'India: Government Economic Survey Presents case for Basic Income', BIEN, 4 February.

Part I

[1] Wadhwa, V. (2015) 'Sorry but the jobless future isn't a luddite fallacy', *Washington Post*, 7 July.

[2] Rodriguez-Montemayor R. (2016) 'How to share the benefits of technology', INSEAD Knowledge, 11 May, knowledge.insead.edu/blog/insead-blog/how-to-share-the-benefits-of-technology-4678.

[3] *The Economist* (2016) 'Rethinking the welfare state: basically flawed', 4 June, economist.com/news/leaders/21699907-proponents-basic-income-underestimate-how-disruptive-it-would-be-basically-flawed.

[4] Van Parijs, P. (1998) *Real Freedom for All: What (if Anything) can Justify Capitalism?*, Oxford, Oxford University Press.

[5] See Bianchi, M. and Bobba, M. (2013) 'Liquidity, risk, and occupational choices', *Review of Economic Studies*, 80(2), pp 491–511.

[6] Banerjee, A., Hanna, R., Kreindler, G. and Olken, B. (2015) 'Debunking the stereotype of the lazy welfare recipient: evidence from cash transfer programs worldwide', CID Working Paper No. 308, Center for International Development, Harvard University.

[7] See, for instance, the evidence on the impact of food stamps in the US – Williamson Hoynes, H. and Whitmore Schanzenbach, D. (2012) 'Work incentives and the Food Stamp program', *Journal of Public Economics*, 96(1–2), pp 151–62.

[8] *The Economist* (2015), 'Basically Unaffordable', 23 May, economist.com/news/finance-and-economics/21651897-replacing-welfare-payments-basic-income-all-alluring.

[9] Sandbu, M. (2016) 'Free Lunch: An affordable Utopia', *Financial Times*, 7 June.

[10] Sandbu, M. (2016) 'Free Lunch: Radically misunderstood: gainsaying the naysayers on universal basic income', *Financial Times*, 22 July.

[11] See, for example, Van Parijs, P. and Vanderborght Y. (2017) *Basic Income: a radical proposal for a free society and a sane economy*, Cambridge, MA: Harvard University Press.

12 Evans, P. and Rodriguez-Montemayor, E. (2017) 'Are we prepared for the talent overhaul induced by technology?' A GTCI research commentary, Chapter 6, *The Global Talent Competitiveness Index 2017*, gtci2017.com/documents/GTCI_2017_web_r5.pdf.

13 Innovators and top inventors do react to higher taxes. See Akcigit, U., Baslandze, S. and Stantcheva, S. (2016) 'Taxation and the international mobility of inventors', *American Economic Review*, 106(10), pp 2930–81.

14 See, for example, Lansley, S. (2016) *How Social Wealth Funds Can Reduce Inequality and Help Balance the Books*, Bristol: Policy Press.

15 McFarland, K. (2017), 'Amartya Sen: India Not Ready for Basic Income', Basic Income Earth Network, 6 March

16 O'Connell, M. (1993) 'Coming Unfringed: The Unraveling of Job-Based Entitlements', *The American Prospect*, prospect.org/article/coming-unfringed-unraveling-job-based-entitlements.

17 Bremmer, I. (2016) 'These 5 Facts Explain the Unstable Global Middle Class', *Time*, 29 July, time.com/4198164/these-5-facts-explain-the-unstable-global-middle-class.

18 Proctor, B., Semega, J. and Kollar, M. (2016) 'Income and Poverty in the United States: 2015 – Current Population Reports', September, census.gov/content/dam/Census/library/publications/2016/demo/p60-256.pdf.

19 Vogel, P. (2016) 'The Future of Work?', *Global Focus*, globalfocusmagazine.com/the-future-of-work/.

20 Scharf, K. and Smith, S. (2016) 'Peer-to-peer fundraising and 'relational altruism' in charitable giving', VOX, 16 September, voxeu.org/article/peer-peer-fundraising-and-relational-altruism-charitable-giving.

21 DeLong, B. (2016) 'Musings on "Just Deserts" and the Opening of Plato's Republic', bradford-delong.com/2016/09/musings-on-just-deserts-and-the-opening-of-platos-republic-greg-mankiw-defending-the-1-proposes-what-he-cal.html.

22 Belik, V. (2011) 'A Town Without Poverty?', *The Dominion*, 5 September, dominionpaper.ca/articles/4100.

23 Lorenzetti, L. (2015) 'Here's why Turing Pharmaceuticals says 5,000% price bump is necessary', *Fortune*, 21 September, fortune.com/2015/09/21/turing-pharmaceuticals-martin-shkreli-response; Associated Press (2016) 'Turing execs warned Martin Shkreli against price hike, lawyer says', STAT, 17 March, statnews.com/2016/03/17/martin-shkreli-turing-daraprim.

24 Richardson Voyles, L. (2016) 'The EpiPen boss tried to defend price hikes to Congress. No one bought it', *Guardian*, 22 September, theguardian.com/commentisfree/2016/sep/22/epipen-maylan-ceo-defend-price-hikes-congress-heather-bresch.

25 Waring, M. (1988) *Counting for Nothing – what men value and what women are worth*, Toronto: Toronto University Press.

26 Katada, K. (2011) 'Beyond the three selections principle of welfare policy: work, family and belonging', in Verderborght, Y. and Yamamori, T. (eds) *Prospects for a Radical Idea in a Transforming Welfare State*, New York: Palgrave Macmillan.

27 Orloff, A.S. (with Julia O'Connor and Sheila Shaver) (1999) *States, Markets, Families: Gender, Liberalism and Social Policy in Australia, Canada, Great Britain and the United States*, Cambridge: Cambridge University Press; Robeyns, I. (2000) 'Hush money or emancipation fee? A gender analysis of basic income', in van der Veen, R. and Groot, L. (eds) *Basic income on the Agenda: Policy Objectives and Political Chances*, Amsterdam: Amsterdam University Press.

28 Zelleke, A. (2008) 'Should Feminists Endorse a Basic Income? Institutionalizing the Universal Caregiver through an Unconditional Basic Income', paper presented at the 12th Basic Income Earth Network Congress, Dublin, Ireland; McKay, A. (2005) *The Future of Social Security Policy: Women, Work and a Citizens' Basic Income*, Abingdon: Routledge; Pateman, C. (2004) 'Democratizing Citizenship: Some Advantages of a Basic Income', *Politics and Society*, 32; Robeyns (2000); Parker, H. (1991) 'Basic Income and the Labour Market', Basic Income Research Group, Discussion Paper No. 1.

29 Baker, J. (2008) 'All things considered, should feminists embrace basic income?', *Basic Income Journal*, 3(3).

30 Zelleke (2008).

31 Pateman (2004).

32 Srnicek, N. and Williams, A. (2015) *Inventing the Future*, London: Verso.

33 Commission on Social Justice (1994) *Social Justice: Strategies for Renewal*, London: Vintage; Atkinson, A.B. (2015) *Inequality*, Cambridge, MA: Harvard University Press.

34 Reed, H. and Lansley, S. (2016) *Universal Basic Income: An idea whose time has come?* London: Compass, p 10.

35 Orton, M. (2015) *Something's Not Right*, London: Compass.

36 Work and Pensions Select Committee (2017) *Citizen's Income*, HC 793, House of Commons, p 8.

37 Marshall, T.H. (1952) *Citizenship and Social Class*, Cambridge: Cambridge University Press, p 11.

Part II

1 Ministry of Social Affairs and Health (2016) 'Ministry of Social Affairs and Health requests opinions on a basic income experiment', press release, 25 August.

2 Simon, H. (2000) 'A Basic Income for All, A Forum Response', *Boston Review*, bostonreview.net/forum/basic-income-all/herbert-simon-ubi-and-flat-tax.

3 Brynjolffson, E., McAfee, A. and Spence, M. (2014) 'New World Order: Labor, Capital, and Ideas in the Power Law Economy', Foreign Affairs, July/August, foreignaffairs.com/articles/united-states/2014-06-04/new-world-order.

4 *The Leap Manifesto*, leapmanifesto.org/en/the-leap-manifesto.

5   Monsebraaten, L. (2016) 'Ontario's soaring poverty gap 'starkest' for single adults as welfare rates stagnate', *Toronto Star*, 9 May thestar.com/news/gta/2016/05/09/ontarios-poverty-gap-soars-as-welfare-rates-stagnate.html.

6   Forget, E.L. (2011) 'The Town with No Poverty: The Health Effects of a Canadian Guaranteed Annual Income Field Experiment', *Canadian Public Policy*, 37(3), pp 282–305, researchgate.net/publication/227387994_The_Town_with_No_Poverty_The_Health_Effects_of_a_Canadian_Guaranteed_Annual_Income_Field_Experiment.

7   Goar, C. (2011) 'Anti-poverty success airbrushed out', *Toronto Star*, 11 January, thestar.com/opinion/editorialopinion/2011/01/11/goar_antipoverty_success_airbrushed_out.html.

8   The Angus Reid Institute (2016) 'Basic Income? Basically unaffordable, say most Canadians', Angus Reid Institute, 11 August, angusreid.org/guaranteed-income.

9   Whitfield, E. (2016) 'Democratizing Wealth: A Next System Model for the US South and Beyond', The Next System Project, 10 August, thenextsystem.org/democratizing-wealth-a-next-system-model-for-the-us-south-and-beyond/.

10   Himelfarb, A. and Hennessy, T. (2016) 'Basic Income: Rethinking Social Policy', Canadian Centre for Policy Alternatives, Ontario, policyalternatives.ca/sites/default/files/uploads/publications/National%20Office%2C%20Ontario%20Office/2016/10/CCPA%20ON%20Basic%20Income_FINAL.pdf.

11   Caffin, B. (2016) 'With experiments springing up around the world, 2016 will be the year basic income is put to the test', Nesta, nesta.org.uk/2016-predictions/universal-basic-income.

12   Maslow, A.H. (1987) *Motivation and Personality* (3rd edition), New York: Harper & Row.

13   Mulgan G., (2016) 'Help Us Find 2016's New Radicals', Nesta, 14 February, nesta.org.uk/blog/help-us-find-2016s-new-radicals.

14   Crabtree, S. (2013) 'State of the Global Workplace' Gallup, 8 October, gallup.com/poll/165269/worldwide-employees-engaged-work.aspx.

15   See, for example, Black, B. (1986) 'The Abolition of Work', in *The Abolition of Work and Other Essays*, Loompanics Unlimited.

16   Graeber, D. (2013) 'On the Phenomenon of Bullshit Jobs', *Strike! Magazine*, strikemag.org/bullshit-jobs/.

17   Morris, W. and Briggs, A. (1962) *William Morris: Selected Writings and Designs*, Harmondsworth: Pelican.

18   New Economics Foundation (2010) '21 Hours: the case for a shorter working week', 13 February, neweconomics.org/21-hours/.

19   Srnicek, N. and Williams, A. (2015) *Inventing the Future*, London: Verso.

20   Lansley, S. (2016) *A Sharing Economy: How Social Wealth Funds Can Reduce Inequality and Help Balance the Books*, Bristol, UK: Policy Press, pp 50-1.

21   Reynolds, J. (2016) 'How I learnt to stop worrying and love basic income', *New Statesman*, 17 February.

22   Dansk Arbejdsgiverforening (DA) 'Flexicurity in Denmark', da.dk/bilag/Flexicurity%20in%20Denmark.pdf.

Part III

[1]   Van Parijs, P. (2016)' Basic Income and Social Democracy', *Social Europe*, 11 April, socialeurope.eu/44878.

[2]   Point I, *ILO Declaration of Philadelphia*, blue.lim.ilo.org/cariblex/pdfs/ILO_dec_philadelphia.pdf.

[3]   Mestrum, F. (2016) *The Social Commons: Rethinking Social Justice in Post-Neoliberal Societies*, Petaling Jaya, Malaysia; socialcommons.eu.

[4]   *Guardian* (2016) 'The Guardian view on a universal income: the high price of free money', Editorial, 6 June, theguardian.com/commentisfree/2016/jun/06/the-guardian-view-on-a-universal-income-the-high-price-of-free-money.

[5]   Deutscher Bundestag (2013), Problematische Auswirkungen auf Arbeitsanreize', bundestag.de/dokumente/textarchiv/2010/31904334_kw45_pa_petitionen/203030.

[6]   Torry, M. (2013) *Money For Everyone: Why we need a citizen's income*, Bristol: Policy Press.

[7]   Campbell, J. and Oliver, M. (1996) *Disability Politics: Understanding Our Past, Changing Our Future*, London: Routledge; Oliver, M. and Barnes, C. (2012) *The New Politics Of Disablement*, Basingstoke: Palgrave Macmillan.

[8]   See: madstudies2014.wordpress.com.

[9]   Beresford, P. (2008) 'Welfare Users And Social Policy', in Alcock, P., May, M. and Rowlingson, K. (eds) *The Student's Companion to Social Policy*, 3rd edition, Oxford: Blackwell Publishing, pp 259–66.

[10] Oliver, M. (1996) *Understanding Disability: From theory to practice*, Basingstoke: Macmillan.

[11] Beresford, P. (2016) *All Our Welfare: Towards participatory social policy*, Bristol: Policy Press.

[12] Beresford (2016).

[13] Beresford (2016).

[14] Allen, J.T. (2002) 'Negative Income Tax', *The Concise Encyclopedia of Economics*, Library of Economics and Liberty, econlib.org/library/Enc1/NegativeIncomeTax.html.

Part IV

[1]   On the history of basic income proposals, see Van Parijs, P. and Vanderborght, Y. (2017) *Basic Income. A radical proposal for a free society and a sane economy*, Cambridge, MA: Harvard University Press, Chapter 4.

[2]   Is there any indication that it will? Here is one, taken from the transcript of an interview with Yanis Varoufakis in *The Economist*, on March 31st 2016, found at economist.com/ESDvaroufakis:

'The basic income approach is absolutely essential, but it is not part of the social democratic tradition. Think about it. The post-war consensus was all about national insurance, it was not about basic income. Now, either

Notes

we are going to have a basic income that regulates this new society of ours, or we are going to have very substantial social conflicts.'
See Van Parijs and Vanderborght (2017), Chapter 7, for an overview of political support in the various political families.

3   Cunliffe, J. and Erreygers, G. (eds) (2004) *The Origins of Universal Grants*, Basingstoke: Palgrave Macmillan, pp 3-16, 81-91.

4   For a detailed history, see Torry, M. (2013) *Money for Everyone*, Bristol, Policy Press, pp 17-42.

5   Williams, J.R. (1943) *Something to Look Forward to*, London: MacDonald and Co.

6   House of Commons Treasury and Civil Service Committee (1982) *The Structure of Personal Income Taxation and Income Support: Minutes of Evidence*, HC 331-ix, London: Her Majesty's Stationery Office, p 459.

7   House of Commons Treasury and Civil Service Committee (1983) *Enquiry into the Structure of Personal Income Taxation and Income Support*, Third Special Report, Session 1982-3, section 13.35, quoted in Parker, H. (1989) *Instead of the Dole: An enquiry into integration of the tax and benefit systems*, London: Routledge, p 100.

8   Macnicol, J. (1980) *The Movement for Family Allowances, 1918-1945: A Study in Social Policy Development*, London: Heinemann.

9   Torry (2013).

10 Painter, A. and Thoung, C. (2015) *Report: Creative citizen, creative state – The principled and pragmatic case for a Universal Basic Income,* London: Royal Society of Arts; Reed, H. and Lansley, S. (2016) *Universal Basic Income: An idea whose time has come*, London: Compass; Standing, G., (2017) *Basic Income: And how we can make it happen*, London, Penguin Random House; Van Parijs, and Vanderborght (2017); Miller, A., *A Basic Income handbook*, Edinburgh: Luath Press; Torry, M. (2016) *The Feasibility of Citizen's Income*, New York: Palgrave Macmillan; Torry, M. (forthcoming) *Why we need a Citizen's Basic Income*, Bristol: Policy Press. At a seminar at LSE in November 2016 Professor David Piachaud – not an advocate of citizen's basic income – credited my books as being a significant factor in the increasing interest in citizen's basic income. I shall leave it to the reader to decide whether there is in any validity in his suggestion.

11 Torry, M. (2017) *A variety of indicators evaluated for two implementation methods for a Citizen's Basic Income*, Euromod Working Paper EM 12/17, Colchester: Institute for Social and Economic Research, iser.essex.ac.uk/research/publications/working-papers/euromod/em12-17.

12 Torry (2016) *The Feasibility of Citizen's Income*.

13 Torry, M. (2016) *How might we implement a Citizen's Income?*, London: Institute for Chartered Accountants of England and Wales, http://citizensincome.org/news/icaew-report-on-implementing-citizens-income/

14 Torry, M. (2013), pp 22-7; Torry (2016) *The Feasibility of Citizen's Income*, pp 238-9.

15 As critiqued in Haagh, L. (2011) 'Basic Income, Social Democracy and Control over Time', *Policy and Politics*, 39(1), pp 41-64 and Haagh, L. (2015) 'Alternative Social States and the Basic Income Debate: Institutions,

211

Inequality and Human Development', *Basic Income Studies*, 10(1), Special
Issue on Thomas Piketty's *Capital in the Twenty-First Century*, degruyter.com/
view/j/bis.ahead-of-print/bis-2015-0002/bis-2015-0002.xml.

[16] Zuckerberg, M. (2017) Facebook entry, 5 July.

[17] Zuckerberg, in reference to the Alaskan Dividend Fund, noted it as
an advantage that the dividend (of a very modest value in subsistence
sufficiency terms – $1,000 p.a.) was 'funded by natural resources rather
than raising taxes'. And he noted, as a 'novel approach' to basic income,
how this model 'comes from conservative principles of smaller government,
rather than progressive principles of a larger safety net'. Zuckerberg in effect
questioned the sufficiency of a basic income by commenting, 'most effective
safety net programs create an incentive or *need* to work rather than just giving
a handout.'

[18] He cited the example of 'subsistence fishing' whereby the government
distributes fish to enable locals to harvest fish and subsist. Zuckerberg
linked the private management of Native Corporations that pay dividends
to an alternative form of basic income to one paid through state-organised
systems.

[19] Haagh, L. (forthcoming) 'Public Ownership within Varieties of Capitalism:
Regulatory Foundations for Welfare and Freedom', *International Journal of
Public Policy*.

[20] Haagh, L. (2017) 'Basic Income should be seen as a Democratic Right, not a
Solution to Unemployment', *Royal Society of Arts Journal*, March, and Haagh,
L. (2017) 'Basic Income as a Pivoting Reform', *Nature Human Behaviour*,
Article 0125, June.

[21] Haagh, L. (2017) 'Basic Income and Institutional Transformation', *Compass*,
2 March. Reproduced as 'Basic Income's Radical Role', *Social Europe*, www.
socialeurope.eu/basic-incomes-radical-role

[22] Coyle, D. (2014) *GDP – A Brief but Affectionate History*, Princeton University
Press.

[23] Hirschman, A.O. (1970) *Exit, Voice and Loyalty*, Cambridge, MA: Harvard
University Press.

[24] Haagh (forthcoming).

[25] Haagh (2011).

[26] In a radio debate on Danish R1 on basic income on 5 August 2017, in which
I participated, the Danish social scientist Jørn Loftager also made this point.
The member of parliament and shadow spokesperson for social affairs for
the Alternativet, Torsten Gejl, with whom I shared in a public debate on the
topic in March 2017 in Copenhagen, observed he owed his career to the
effectively (if not literally) lax conditions on basic income support in the
1980s, as it allowed him time to find his way in life.

[27] Haagh (2015).

[28] Haagh (forthcoming).

[29] Atkinson A.B (2014), *Inequality: What Can Be Done?*, Cambridge, MA:
Harvard University Press, Chapter 8.

[30] Hirschman (1970).

31 Sunstein, C.R. (2009) *Laws of Fear*, Cambridge: Cambridge University Press, pp 181–5.
32 This was well illustrated in a testimony to the UK Work and Pensions Committee Inquiry into Citizens' Income – Oral Evidence Session, 12 January 2017, data.parliament.uk/writtenevidence/committeeevidence.svc/evidencedocument/work-and-pensions-committee/universal-basic-income/oral/45336.pdf by the representative of Unison, Becca Kirkpatrick, UNISON West Midlands Community Branch, when she explained she was unable to care for her relative given conditionality policies.
33 Suplicy, E. (2002) *Renda de Cidadania*, São Paulo: Cortez Editora.
34 Haagh (forthcoming).
35 Davala, S., Jhabvala, R., Mehta S.K. and Standing G. (2015) *Basic Income: A Transformative Policy for India*, London and New Delhi: Bloomsbury, pp 31–70.
36 Three and a half bighas make one acre.
37 Davala, Jhabvala, Mehta and Standing (2015).
38 Mackenzie, J., Mathers, S., Mawdsley, G. and Payne, A. (2016) *The Basic Income Guarantee*, Edinburgh: Reform Scotland.
39 Evans, M. (2015) *Fairness Matters*, Fife: The Fairer Fife Commission, pp 6, 25.
40 Rothbard, M.N. (1973) 'For a New Liberty The Libertarian Manifesto', Ludwig von Mises Institute, Auburn, Alabama, 20 July, mises.org/library/new-liberty-libertarian-manifesto.
41 Zwolinski, M. (2015) 'Libertarianism and the Welfare State', 20 August, academia.edu/23843573/Libertarianism_and_the_Welfare_State.
42 Spencer, H. (1851) *Social Statics: or, The Conditions essential to Human Happiness specified, and the First of Them Developed*, London: John Chapman.
43 George, H. (1879) *Progress and Poverty*, New York: D. Appleton & Company.
44 Hayek, F. (1978) *The Constitution of Liberty*, The University of Chicago Press.
45 Zwolinski, M. (2013) 'Why Did Hayek Support a Basic Income?', Libertarianism.org, 23 December, libertarianism.org/columns/why-did-hayek-support-basic-income.
46 See the 1968 interview (from 'Firing Line with William F Buckley Jr') in which Milton Friedman explained the negative income tax: youtube.com/watch?v=xtpgkX588nM.
47 Murray, C. (2006) *In Our Hands: A Plan to Replace the Welfare State*, American Enterprise Institute Press.
48 Reed, H. and Lansley, S. (2016) *A Universal Basic Income: An Idea Whose Time Has Come?* London: Compass, Appendix B, compassonline.org.uk/wp-content/uploads/2016/05/UniversalBasicIncomeByCompass-Spreads.pdf.
49 Harrop, A. (2016) *For Us All: redesigning social security, for the 2020s*, London: Fabian Society.
50 Mian, E. (2016) 'Don't fall for universal basic income: it's a utopian fiction that wastes public money on the rich', *Independent*, 22 March, independent.co.uk/voices/don-t-fall-for-universal-basic-income-it-s-a-utopian-fiction-that-wastes-public-money-on-the-rich-a6945881.html.
51 Reed and Lansley (2016).

[52] There are other ways of defining a 'full scheme'. For example, it could be defined as a scheme with payments set at levels sufficient to provide a minimum acceptable living standard and/or that abolishes all means-tested benefits, not just a majority. Such a scheme might be described, alternatively, as a 'pure UBI'.

[53] 1961 is the earliest year for which trend data is available: Institute for Fiscal Studies, 'Incomes in the UK', ifs.org.uk/tools_and_resources/incomes_in_uk.

[54] For example, the full cost to the Exchequer of the provision of tax relief on pension contributions is £34.3bn (around £10bn if such relief was restricted to the standard rate of income tax). Thurley, D. (2016) *Restricting Pension Tax Relief*, House of Commons Library, Briefing Paper SN-05091, 22 November, researchbriefings.files.parliament.uk/documents/SN05901/SN05901.pdf.

[55] Painter and Thoung (2015).

Part V

[1] See Lehto, O. (2017) 'Comments on Jacobin's "The UBI Bait and Switch"', BIEN Basic Income News, 30 January, basicincome.org/news/2017/01/comments-on-jacobins/.

[2] The Green Party model: vihreat.fi/asiat/vihrea-politiikka/teemat/koyhyys/.perustulo; The Left Alliance model: vasemmistonperustulo.wordpress.com; The Libera model: libera.fi/wpcontent/uploads/2013/12/Perustili_EN_131210b.pdf; The Sitra/Tänk proposal: sitra.fi/uutiset/ajatushautomo-tank-kenttakoe-paras-tapa-kokeilla-perustuloa.

[3] 'Objectives and implementation of the Basic Income Experiment', Kela, kela.fi/web/en/basic-income-objectives-and-implementation.

[4] Jauhiainen, A. and Mäkinen, J.H. (2017) 'Why Finland's Basic Income Experiment Isn't Working', *New York Times*, 20 July, nytimes.com/2017/07/20/opinion/finland-universal-basic-income.html.

[5] I have argued elsewhere (Lehto, 2017) that the experiment is 'built upon the sorrowful soil of a Protestant work ethic that fetishises work incentives and bemoans the metaphysical sinfulness of laziness.'

[6] Lehto, O. (forthcoming) 'Basic Income Around the World: The Unexpected Benefits of Unconditional Cash Transfers', a Research Paper for the Adam Smith Institute; De Wispelaere, J. (2015) 'An Income of One's Own: The Political Analysis of Universal Basic Income', Acta Universitatis Tamperensis 2121, Finland: University of Tampere Press, urn.fi/URN:ISBN:978-951-44-9989-0.

[7] Weller, C. (2017) 'Finland's basic income experiment is already lowering stress levels — and it's only 4 months old', *Business Insider*, 10 May, businessinsider.com/finland-basic-income-less-stress-2017-5?r=US&IR=T&IR=T.

[8] McFarland, K. (2017) 'Finland: First Results from Pilot Study? Not Exactly', BIEN Basic Income News, 10 May, basicincome.org/news/2017/05/finland-first-results-basic-income-pilot-not-exactly.

9   MacDonald, V. (2016) 'Health Unit supports guaranteed income',
    Northumberlandtoday.com, 26 June, northumberlandtoday.
    com/2016/06/26/health-unit-supports-guaranteed-income; Migneault, J.
    (2016) 'Health Unit: Lift more people out of poverty with a basic income
    guarantee', Sudbury.com, 25 April, sudbury.com/local-news/health-unit-lift-
    more-people-out-of-poverty-with-a-basic-income-guarantee-285837.

10 Simcoe Muskoka District Health Unit, 'Public Health Support for a Basic
    Income Guarantee', alPHa RESOLUTION A15-4, c.ymcdn.com/sites/
    alphaweb.site-ym.com/resource/collection/CE7462B3-647D-4394-8071-
    45114EAAB93C/A15-4_Basic_Income_Guarantee.pdf.

11 Moore, K. and Ontario Medical Association (2015) 'National Support for a
    Basic Income Guarantee', 2015 CMA Resolution, alphaweb.org/resource/
    resmgr/Resolutions/CMA_BIG_Resolution_2015.pdf.

12 Blais, F. (2002) *Ending poverty: A basic income for all Canadians*, Toronto:
    James Lorimer & Company.

13 See basisinkomen.nl/peiling-hond-basisinkomen-40100.

14 TV programme: WNL-Nieuwsmakers Annemarie van Gaal, 28 March 2017.

15 Standing, G. (2017) *Basic Income: and how we can make it happen*, London:
    Penguin, pp 265–6.

16 Pew Research Center (2015) *The American Middle Class is Losing Ground*,
    Washington, DC: Pew Research Center.

17 Proctor, B.D., Semega, J.L. and Kollar, M.A. (2016), 'Income and Poverty
    in the United States: 2015 – Current Population Reports', US Census
    Bureau, September, P60-256(RV), census.gov/content/dam/Census/library/
    publications/2016/demo/p60-256.pdf.

18 *The Economist* (2012) 'Free exchange: hope springs a trap', 12 May,
    economist.com/node/21554506.

19 Information on the calculation used to determine the payment level is
    available at eight.world.

20 See 'Will saving poor children lead to overpopulation?' Gapminder,
    gapminder.org/videos/will-saving-poor-children-lead-to-overpopulation.

21 More information on this calculation is available at eight.world.

22 Haushofer, J. and Dhapiro, J. (2016) 'The short-term impact of
    unconditional cash transfers to the poor. Experimental evidence from
    Kenya', *Quarterly Journal of Economics*, 131(4), pp 1973–2042.

23 Brancaglione, M. (2016) 'Robinright: an intellectual property license
    inspired by basic income', 2 March, medium.com/marcus-brancaglione/
    robinright-an-intellectual-property-license-inspired-by-basic-income-
    60cc26ea30f9.

Part VI

1   OECD (2017) *Basic Income As a Policy Option, Can It Add Up?* Paris: OECD.

2   Van Parijs, P. and Vanderborght, Y. (2017) *Basic Income. A Radical Proposal
    for a Free Society and a Sane Economy,* Cambridge, MA: Harvard University
    Press, pp 165–7.

3   Bowman, D., Mallett, S. and Cooney-O'Donoghue, F. (2017) 'Basic Income: trade-offs and bottom lines', Working Paper, Research & Policy Centre, Fitzroy, VIC, Australia: Brotherhood of St Laurence.

4   Roberts, R. (2017) 'Indian politicians consider universal basic income following successful trials', *Independent*, 28 July, independent.co.uk/news/world/politics/ndia-politician-universal-basic-income-trials-discuss-poverty-employment-a7865541.html.

5   Painter, A. and Thoung, C. (2015) *Creative Citizen, Creative State: the Principled and Pragmatic Case for a Universal Basic Income*, London: Royal Society for the Encouragement of Arts, Manufactures and Commerce; Reed, H. and Lansley, S. (2016) *A Universal Basic Income, An Idea Whose Time Has Come?* Compass; Andrews, K. (2015) 'Reform tax credits with a negative income tax, says new report', press release, 26 October, Adam Smith Institute, adamsmith.org/news/press-release-reform-tax-credits-with-a-negative-income-tax-says-new-report. For alternative proposals, see 'Current schemes', Basic Income UK, basicincome.org.uk/current_schemes

6   'Citizen's income inquiry', parliament.uk/business/committees/committees-a-z/commons-select/work-and-pensions-committee/inquiries/parliament-2015/citizens-income-16-17; 'Social Security Committee – Agenda Thursday 9 March 2017', parliament.scot/S5_Social_Security/Meeting%20Papers/PublicPapers_20170309.pdf.

7   Liberal Democrat Voice (2016) 'What party members think about a universal basic income and benefits sanctions', libdemvoice.org/what-party-members-think-about-a-universal-basic-income-and-benefits-sanctions-51889.html.

8   Cruddas, J. and Kibasi, T. (2016) 'A Universal Basic Mistake', *Prospect*, July.

9   Schifferes, S. (2017) 'How inequality became the big issue troubling the world's top economists', *The Conversation*, theconversation.com/how-inequality-became-the-big-issue-troubling-the-worlds-top-economists-83171

Index